FAVORITE PERENNIAL FLOWERS

Distributed by
WALDEN BOOKS • RESALE DIVISION
Stamford, Conn.
Published by OTTENHEIMER PUBLISHERS, INC.

Picture Credits

A-Z Tourist Photo Library: pages 13, 50, 71, 75
Bernard Alfieri: pages 68, 69
H. R. Allen: pages 68, 90
Alpine Garden Society: page 35
D. C. Arminson: pages 18, 93
K. A. Beckett: pages 69, 74
Carlo Bevilacqua: page 75
Antony Birks: page 66
Blackmore & Langdon: page 34
Arthur Boarder: page 41
R. J. Corbin: pages 4, 5, 22, 24, 25, 26, 27 28, 29, 30, 52, 55, 61, 68, 73, 77, 78, 79 80, 83, 86
J. E. Downward: pages 11, 14, 44, 51
Valerie Finnis: pages 12, 13, 14, 16, 17, 23 35, 39, 40, 45, 48, 49, 52, 57, 61, 64, 67 69, 70, 78, 81, 88, 94
A. P. Hamilton: page 63
Iris Hardwick: pages 9, 20, 88
Ron Hatfield: page 22
Peter Hunt: pages 7, 8, 15, 17, 20, 21, 43 44, 45, 51, 53, 54, 55, 61, 85

A. J. Huxley: pages 51, 93
George E. Hyde: pages 18, 62, 71, 89
Leslie Johns: pages 6, 16, 20, 65
Reginald Kaye: page 65
Edna Knowles: page 76
John Markham: pages 37, 58, 74, 97
Elsa Megson: pages 55, 67, 68, 73, 86, 87 88, 94
Opera Mundi: page 38
Ronald Parrett: pages 32, 33, 61
Ray Proctor: page 62
Peter Russell: page 57
Harry Smith: pages 8, 10, 19, 31, 36, 37, 38 41, 42, 43, 44, 45, 46, 47, 48, 49, 50, 54 55, 56, 59, 60, 62, 63, 64, 66, 67, 68, 69 71, 75, 76, 80, 81, 82, 85, 87, 89, 90, 91 92, 95, 96
A. Twiner: page 15
D. S. Whicker: page 72
D. Wildridge: page 95
Henry Wood: pages 74, 75
Dennis Woodland: pages 58, 85

Horticultural Consultants: Dr. Conrad B. Link and Dr. Francis C. Stark, Professors of Horticulture, University of Maryland, College Park.
The material in this book was first published by Marshall Cavendish Ltd. of London, in *Encyclopedia of Gardening.* The British flavor of the text is unmistakable, but the horticultural consultants have endeavored to adapt the cultural and hardiness recommendations to the United States. Botanical names have been checked against many sources, using Bailey and Bailey, *Hortus Second* as the final authority. Even so, some names used have been retained even though they appear in none of our sources.
The American gardener is cautioned that many of the species mentioned, and especially the varieties and cultivars, may not be available in the United States.

Copyright © 1976 Ottenheimer Publishers, Inc.
© Marshall Cavendish Limited 1968—69—70—73
This material was first published by Marshall Cavendish Limited in *Encyclopedia of Gardening*

Introduction

Of the numerous flowering plants cultivated throughout the world, perennials are probably the most varied. Ranging from low-growing ground covers to giant hollyhocks, from dwarf flowers for the rock garden to spreading shrub-like bushes, herbaceous perennials are the favorite bedding plants of gardeners everywhere.

Favorite Perennial Flowers is a complete guide to popular hardy flowering plants. More than 100 kinds of perennials are listed in alphabetical order for easy reference, with hints for their successful cultivation and examples in color on every page. As well as general information about perennials, there are special sections for the gardener who wants additional information about the cultivation of such popular flowers as dahlias, delphiniums, irises, peonies and pelargonium.

Contents

PERENNIALS

This term is used to describe a plant which does not die after flowering, but persists for a number of years, in contrast with an annual which flowers once and then dies after setting seed, and a biennial which completes its life cycle in two years. The term 'perennial' may properly be applied to shrubs and trees but is more often used in conjunction with the term 'hardy herbaceous' to describe the plants which form the mainstay of herbaceous borders, though they are often grown in other parts of the garden, either in company with other plants or as isolated specimens. Though the term is applied to plants which live for more than 2 years, many perennials live for many years and such plants as herbaceous peonies and the oriental poppy (*Papaver orientale*) are particularly long lived. By contrast some perennial plants, for instance lupins, may have a life span of only five or six years.

Monocarpic plants Although the literal meaning is 'once fruiting', as far as gardeners are concerned, plants which take an indefinite period to reach their flowering age and die immediately afterwards are said to be monocarpic. They represent only a small number of plants, but examples familiar to many gardeners include some meconopsis species, *Saxifraga longifolia*, *Saxifraga* 'Tumbling Waters', houseleeks (sempervivums), most bromeliads, and the so-called century plant, *Agave americana*, which, although it does not take a hundred years to flower and then die, may well take over fifty years.

Planting perennials With herbaceous plants, one of the problems is not so much *how* to plant them as *when*. The vast majority of border plants are pretty tough and perennials such as Michaelmas or Shasta daisies will quickly take root and establish themselves even if they are left lying on the soil surface. Most border plants, too, can be planted, weather and soil conditions permitting, at any time from September to March. But there is an important minority which planted in autumn, seem unable to survive their first winter. Catmint *(Nepeta cataria)* is one of the classic examples, a characteristic that is shared by other grey and silver leaved perennials. Reputable nurserymen will automatically defer delivery of this kind of plant until early spring, unless grown in containers.

The actual operation of planting perennials is simple and straightforward. Plant-ing with the new season's dormant shoots a few inches below soil level will be satisfactory for most of the better known and more widely grown border plants. Where established clumps are being divided up, it is the younger and more vigorous outside shoots that should be planted.

Herbaceous peonies require very shallow planting; putting them in too deep is one of the main causes of delay in flowering and poor crops of bloom. The dormant eyes, which are easy to distinguish, since they are crimson in color, should not be more than an inch below soil level.

Bearded irises are another group of border plants that require the shallowest of planting. Ideally the rhizomes should actually be resting on the soil with their upper surfaces above ground level, though on light soils, particularly, they may be planted so that the rhizomes are just covered with soil. This covering will gradually be washed away by rain, by which time their roots will have taken hold. They are rather tricky to plant and are easily disturbed by subsequent weeding or cultivating until the fleshy anchoring roots have had a chance to take hold. It is better to keep the hoe or fork well away from them during their first season and carry out any necessary weeding operations by hand.

Herbaceous borders

The herbaceous border, which is a comparative newcomer to the garden scene, is still one of its most popular features. Introduced at the turn of the century as a protest against the monotonous formality of Victorian garden design, its popularity has steadily increased until today there are few gardens without some kind of perennial border to enhance their beauty throughout the months of summer and autumn.

Restricted originally to plants of purely perennial habit — in the main, those whose growth begins afresh from ground level each year — the terms of reference have gradually been extended so that today we find included not only spring and summer bulbs and corms but also small shrubby plants and those curious in-betweens whose woody top growth persists throughout the winter, but which otherwise display most of the characteristics of true perennials. These are the subshrubs, of which plants such as the plumbago flowered *Ceratostigma willmottianum*, *Caryopteris clandonensis*, and the Russian sage, *Perovskia atriplicifolia* are typical examples.

Preparing the site Preliminary preparation of the site for a herbaceous border is of paramount importance. Much of its subsequent success or failure will depend on the thoroughness with which it is carried out. Some soils, of course, are a good deal more difficult to prepare than others, but whether you garden on heavy, back breaking clay or easily managed, well drained sandy loam there must be sufficient supplies of humus in the soil if the plants are to be of their best.

Deep digging and thorough cultivation are two further essentials. Most of the occupants of the border will remain in the same positions for at least three years, while other more permanent specimens such as peonies, hellebores, romneyas and hemerocallis can stay put almost indefinitely, without the necessity for division or replanting.

To make sure that such conditions are fulfilled it may be necessary to double dig the whole of the projected plot. This will result in a thorough breaking up of both the surface and lower layers of soil.

Humus Thorough digging, however, is not sufficient to create the soil conditions in which perennials thrive best. To provide them, plentiful supplies of humus or humus forming material must be present in the soil, enough, in fact, to satisfy much of the plants' needs for several seasons, as normally the border will be due for a complete overhaul only once in every three to four years.

Humus can be provided by a variety of materials, the best of which, of course, is the almost impossible to obtain stable or farmyard manure. Most of us, however, will have to settle for alternatives. Compost, properly made and well rotted down, heads the list of these but supplies of this are quickly exhausted unless we supplement our garden and domestic waste with straw, sawdust, or other similar materials.

Leafmold is excellent, but expensive unless you are lucky enough to have access to natural sources of supply. Oak and beech leaves are the richest in plant foods, while bracken rots down to a material of peat like consistency, good for stepping up the humus content of the soil but otherwise lacking in plant foods. Young bracken shoots, on the other hand, are rich in plant foods and minerals and make a valuable contribution to the compost heap.

For the town gardener and for those who cannot readily obtain the materials mentioned above, peat is the best soil conditioner. It is clean both to store and handle, and can hold many times its own bulk of moisture.

Spent hops are another first-rate humus forming material. If you can obtain supplies in bulk from a local brewery, they will be relatively cheap.

These, or any other similar materials, are best worked into the upper layer as digging progresses. Alternatively they can be forked into the soil a few weeks before the plants are put in.

Fortunately, the vast majority of the more widely grown herbaceous perennials are very accommodating. They will thrive in most types of soil although characteristics such as height, vigor and rate of increase will vary considerably between, for example, light, sandy loams and heavy, sticky clays. It is a good rule never to coddle temperamental plants. There is neither time nor room for them in the herbaceous border, where plants are grown more for their effect in the mass than as individuals.

Weeds The best time of the year to prepare the site for planting is late summer or early autumn. This will give the winter frosts a chance to break up heavy clods to a fine planting tilth. This, of course, is not so important with light sandy soils which can be cultivated at almost any season of the year. As digging progresses, it is imperative to remove every possible vestige of perennial weeds; the aim should be to start with a site that is completely weed free, although when fresh ground is being taken over this can be no more than a counsel of perfection.

Watch particularly for the roots of bindweed, mugwort *(Artemisia vulgaris)* and quack or wine grasses. Any of these can soon stage a rapid comeback even if only a few pieces remain in the soil.

Any of these weeds are anathema in the border and once established will prove well nigh impossible to eradicate without a complete overhaul. Other perennial weeds — not quite as difficult but still a nuisance — include docks, thistles, clover and creeping buttercup. In acid soils sorrel, too, can be troublesome.

If annual weeds multiply alarmingly, and they will in very wet summers, there is no need for undue despondency. Regular sessions with a hand fork or a border fork will keep them in check. Vigorous low growing perennials will act as their own ground cover.

In autumn, and in early spring if possible, the border should have a thorough forking over, removing all perennial weeds. Any clumps of plants that show signs of weed infestation should be dug up. After shaking or washing their roots free of soil, offending weed roots or runners that have penetrated the latter should be carefully teased out and removed. The clumps can then be replanted in the same place, or if their size warrants it, be split up and regrouped. If the replanting is carried out without delay the plants will not suffer any check. In fact, very vigorous growers such as Michaelmas daisies, *Campanula lactiflora* and *Chrysanthemum maximum* will benefit from this procedure.

Weeds are anathema in the border.
1 Trifolium pratense, perennial Clover.
2 Bellis perennia, a wild Daisy.
3 Plantago Major, the Broad-leaved Plantain.

It follows from the foregoing that new stocks received from generous fellow gardeners should have their roots carefully examined for invading weeds before they are planted. We may not be able to suppress entirely the weeds that are present in the soil, but there is no point in deliberately planting trouble.

Supplementary fertilization Unless farmyard manure has been available in generous quantities it will be advisable to give a booster of some kind of fertilizer a few weeks before the border is planted.

Bonemeal and fish meal, which are both organic and slow acting, will give good results, applied at a rate of 2-3 oz to the square yard. As an alternative, a good general fertilizer can be used at the rate recommended by the manufacturers.

A good way of distributing this supplementary plant food is to rake it into the soil when the final preparations for planting are being made. Alternatively, it can be spaded lightly into the surface with a fork. An established border will benefit from a similar application when growth starts in spring.

Location Most of the more widely grown perennials are sun lovers, so that a position facing south or west will be the most suitable for the border. But since this feature is seen at its best when viewed lengthwise, it may be necessary if we plan to enjoy its beauty from some fixed vantage point such as a terrace or the living room windows, to effect some sort of compromise where aspect is concerned.

Generally speaking, any position except a sunless north facing one, or one where the plants suffer shade and drip from overhanging trees, will be quite satisfactory.

Background Just as a fine picture deserves an appropriate frame, so the herbaceous border needs a proper setting for its beauty. In the past this has usually been supplied by a background wall or hedge, but nowadays doublesided and island borders are becoming popular, where the only background is provided by the adjacent grass or paving. Nothing, however, makes a more suitable backcloth than a well kept evergreen hedge — yew, holly, cypress, beech, or hornbeam. Mellowed brick or stone wall, too, can act as a pleasing accompaniment, and even split saplings or bamboo or a wooden fence, when discreetly covered by climbing plants, can provide an attractive setting.

Plants grown against walls or fences will require additional attention where staking and tying are concerned. In rough weather strong gusts and eddies develop at their base which can have disastrous results unless the plants are strongly secured.

Hedges, beautiful though they may be as backgrounds, also have their disadvantages. Most hedging plants are notorious moisture and plant food robbers. Some, such as privet, are much worse than others and should be avoided if a new planting is to be made. The roots of an established hedge can be kept in check by digging a trench a foot or so away from the base of the plants and chopping back all the fibrous roots with a sharp spade. This operation, which should be carried out while the hedge is dormant, could very well coincide with the periodic overhaul and replanting of the border.

If space permits, it is a good plan to leave a gap of 2-3 feet between the foot of the hedge and the rear rank border plants. This, incidentally, will also provide useful access to the back of the border for maintenance work.

Yew is the best plant for a background hedge. Slow and compact in growth, it requires a minimum of attention — one 'top and sides' trim annually will suffice, and its foliage of somber green is the perfect background for the bright colors of the border plants.

Planning Planning the border can be fun. With squared paper and a sheaf of nursery catalogues there could be few pleasanter ways of spending a winter's evening. Ready-made collections complete with planting plans are useful for the complete novice and can form the nucleus of a wider collection, but it is a good deal more interesting to work out your own color schemes and to see the plans coming to fruition in the garden.

There is such a wide choice of herbaceous plants that the permutations and combinations of color, form and texture are infinite in number. Individual tastes vary and so do fashions in flower colors. The pastel shades, popular for so many years, are giving place to the stronger reds, yellows and blues.

A border composed entirely of any one of these primary colors would be striking in its effect, but the planning would need very careful handling and a thorough knowledge of plant characteristics. If you lack experience, you would be well advised to use a mixture of colors, grouped according to your individual taste.

As a general rule, in a border of mixed colors the paler shades should be at each end, with the brighter, more vivid ones grouped mainly at the center. For example, the pure whites of *Phlox paniculata alba*, *Achillea ptarmica* 'The Pearl', and *Gypsophila* 'Bristol Fairy' could melt almost imperceptibly into the cool primrose yellows of *Achillea taygetea* and *Verbascum bombyciferum* (syn. *broussa*), flanked by the deeper yellows of *Hemerocallis* 'Hyperion', one of the best of the free flowering day lilies, and *Lysimachia punctata*, the yellow loose strife.

The middle of the border could explode into brilliant color with scarlet *Lychnis chalcedonica, Lobelia fulgens, Potentilla* 'Gibson's Scarlet', and the garnet red *Astilbe* 'Fanal'. Once past its climax, the border could progress to white once more through the blues of delphiniums, sea holly (*Eryngium maritimum*) whose leaves, as well as the flowers, are metallic blue, and the stately *Echinops ritro,* with thistle like dark green foliage and drumstick flower heads of steely blue. Other suitable blue perennials include the attractive indigo-blue monkshood, *Aconitum* 'Bressingham Spire' and the curious balloon flower, *Platycodon grandiflorum*.

These could be followed by the soft pinks of *Geranium endressii, Sidalcea* 'Sussex Beauty', the long flowering *Veronica spicata* — 'Pavane' and 'Minuet' are both good varieties — and the later blooming ice plant, *Sedum spectabile* 'Brilliant'.

And so back to white again, this time represented by Japanese anemones, *Anemone hupehensis* 'Honorine Jobert', *Lysimachia clethroides, Potentilla alba* and a good garden form of the sweetly scented meadow sweet, *Filipendula ulmaria plena*.

This, of course, would not constitute a complete planting plan, but is merely suggestion that could form the framework of an attractive herbaceous border. Color, though it may be significant in the overall display, is not everything where the successful herbaceous border is concerned. The form and leaf texture of the plants, as well as the manner in which they are grouped, all play a part that is vitally important to the ultimate effect.

It is important to plant in relatively large groups, each restricted to one kind or variety, the size depending on the overall dimensions of the border. Blocks of three plants should, as a general rule, be the minimum, while, for smaller edging and carpeting plants, six would be a reasonable number if spottiness is to be avoided.

Although the general trend should be towards 'shortest in the front, tallest in the rear', this is a rule that should not be too

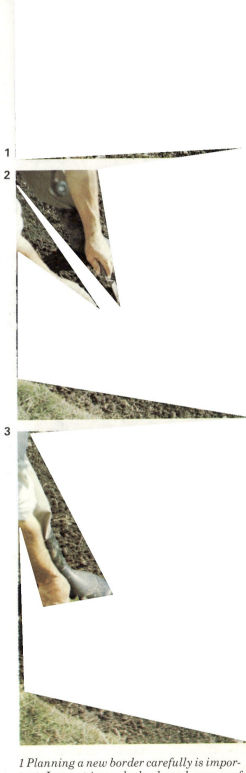

1 *Planning a new border carefully is important. Lay out irregularly shaped groups of plants with adequate space to allow for growth.*
2 *Put the plants into the ground firmly with fine soil around the roots.*
3 *Firm the soil carefully by treading close to the plant, pushing the earth both downward and inward towards the plant.*

5

An established and carefully planned herbaceous border gives an air of permanence to a garden.

sifted compost or a mixture of moist soil and peat that has been kept under cover for this purpose.

With the more vigorous perennials such as golden rod, Shasta daisies, achilleas and campanulas, it is not necessary, if time presses, to be too fussy over planting procedure, provided that the soil has been properly prepared and is in good condition. Others, however, such as peonies, alstroemerias and hellebores will need more careful attention. Peonies, for example, should never be planted with their dormant growth buds more than approximately 2 inches below the surface; planting too deeply is one of the commonest causes of failure to bloom satisfactorily. Late autumn planted specimens frequently fail to survive. This is a rule that might well be applied to all gray leaved border plants. Once established they can tolerate severe weather conditions but in their first winter they often succumb to severe frosts if they are planted in autumn.

For the newcomer to gardening, the importance of dealing only with reputable nurseries and garden centers cannot be overstressed. Their catalogues, in addition to lists and descriptions of plants, will often contain a wealth of information regarding their likes and dislikes. Plants, too, will be delivered at the most appropriate time of year for planting.

Choice of plants Anyone starting an herbaceous border from scratch would be well advised to take advantage of the many new plants and modern varieties of older favorites that require little or no staking and tying. By this means, one of the major summer chores in the border can be considerably reduced.

Many of these new style border plants are entirely self supporting; others need only a few twiggy sticks pushed in among them to keep them in order.

Plants such as tall delphiniums will, of course, have to have each individual flower stem secured to a stake or stout cane. If space permits, it is better to segregate these and other similar top-heavy plants; they do better where they are more easy to get at for maintenance.

Not all the taller border plants suffer from this shortcoming; *Artemisia lactiflora,* for example, is a plant whose 6 foot stems of feathery milk white flowers, smelling like meadowsweet, will stand up to a howling gale without turning a hair, while others, for example the daisies and taller perennial asters, will collapse and sprawl at the first hint of rough weather, if they are not securely staked.

Careful and judicious selection at the planning stage, therefore, can make the border practically trouble free where staking and tying are concerned.

Double sided or 'island' borders achieve similar results in a different way. Plants grown in an open situation are sturdier and more compact than those grown against a wall or hedge which tends to cause them to be drawn both upwards and

rigidly adhered to. Some of the taller plants should be allowed to wander to the middle or even, at certain points, to the front of the border while the lower marginal plants can be permitted to flow unobtrusively inwards to make small pools and rivulets of contrasting height and color among their taller neighbors.

A number of perennials are grown as much for the beauty of their foliage as for the decorative quality of their flowers. Outstanding among these are the hostas, or plantain lilies with their outsize ribbed leaves; acanthus, whose sculptured foliage formed the classic model for the Corinthian capitals of Ancient Greek architecture; hemerocallis, *Iris sibirica* and kniphofias for the contrasting effect of their sword like leaves; the variety of rue known as *Ruta graveolens* 'Jackman's Blue' and others.

Other plants are cultivated for their attractive seed heads. These include the fascinating but invasive Chinese lanterns *(Physalis),* the silvery tasselled *Pulsatilla*

vulgaris or Pasque flower, *Baptisia australis* with its soot like seed pods and the magnificent *Heracleum mantegazzianum,* a garden plant resembling a giant cow parsley whose outsize flat seed heads are borne on stems, 10 feet or more tall.

Planting The great majority of perennial border plants can be planted with safety between the end of September and the last week of March. In fact, the planting of late flowering specimens such as Michaelmas daisies and border chrysanthemums could very well be delayed until April. This varies with local climatic conditions.

Planting holes should be of sufficient depth and breadth to accommodate the roots of the plants without bunching or overcrowding. Small plants can be firmed in by hand, but for large clumps firm with the foot or heel. Although firm planting is desirable, this should not entail embedding the roots in a pocket of sticky 'goo'. In heavy clay soils, planting will have to be delayed until the soil condition improves or, better still, the holes can be filled with

outwards. This sturdier habit makes them less liable to damage by heavy winds and rough weather, and, in addition, access at both sides of the border makes routine maintenance a good deal easier. The idea of a double sided border is not new. Formerly, in large gardens, they were commonly used as a decorative edging in the kitchen garden where they served the dual purpose of screening the vegetable crops and providing flowers for cutting.

One of the attractions of island borders, in addition to ease of maintenance, lies in the fact that they can be viewed from above as well as along their length and from the front. For this reason, the height of the plants should not exceed 3 or 4 feet in order that the kaleidoscope color effects of the plant groupings can be seen to their best advantage.

Prolonging the display One of the main disadvantages of the herbaceous border as a garden feature is the comparatively short time during which it makes a major contribution to the garden display. Normally, it is only in May or June that it really starts to make its color impact, with lupins, oriental poppies, irises, anchusa, aquilegias and other early flowering perennials.

Reaching its peak in July and August, it continues to delight in early autumn and retires in a blaze of fall or perennial aster, red hot pokers, perennial sun flowers and border chrysanthemums, which carry it through, until mid October.

For the other seven months of the year, however, the border can lack color and interest, unless steps are taken to extend its scope by supplementing with others that flower both early and late.

Spring bulbs, such as daffodils, tulips, hyacinths, chionodoxas, scillas and grape hyacinths, will fill the spaces between perennials with bright spring color. A little later, wallflowers, polyanthus, forget-me-nots and other spring bedding plants can be used.

There are a few true herbaceous plants, beginning in January with the hellebores, that in mild climates will considerably extend the border's period of interest and relieve the monotony of bare earth and dead stems. *Helleborus niger,* the Christmas rose, seldom fulfils the promise of its name unless it has the protection of a cold frame or cool greenhouse, but it can be relied on to open its pure white chalices by the end of January. Such structures provide protection for its immaculate petals from damage by wind and rain.

Following close on its heels comes the Lenten rose, *Helleborus orientalis* and other delightful species that include the stately *H. argutifolius* (syn. *H. corsicus)* and *H. foetidus,* whose green flower clusters are a good deal smaller than those of the Corsican types.

In February and March, too, there will be the pink and carmine flower trusses of the bergenias, among the finest of flowering perennials. These useful plants are

Island borders can be viewed from all sides.

outsize members of the saxifrage family and most species are evergreen so that their handsome fleshy leaves, bronze or reddish in winter, as well as their striking flowers, make a valuable contribution to the winter border. 'Ballawley Hybrid', a relatively new introduction from Ireland, is one of the most outstanding examples of the group. Other good forms and species include *B. cordifolia* with rounded crinkly leaves, *B. crassifolia* whose leaves are more spoon shaped than round and *B. schmidtii,* an unusual species the leaves of which have hairy margins and whose loose sprays of clear pink flowers are the earliest to appear.

Blue flowers are always attractive and there are several perennials to provide them once winter is over. The so-called giant forget-me-not, *Brunnera macrophylla* (syn. *Anchusa myosotidiflora*) is one of these, as are the lungworts or pulmonarias. Both of these have foliage that stays attractive throughout the remainder of the season.

There are several species of pulmonaria, the most striking of which is *Pulmonaria angustifolia azurea,* with clear gentian-blue flowers. It looks superb in conjunction with the yellow daisy flowers of the leopard's bane, *Doronicum* 'Harpur Crewe'. *P. angustifolia rubra* has coral-red blossoms, those of *P. saccharata* are pinkish-purple turning to blue, while its strikingly mottled leaves have earned it the popular title of spotted dog. Incidentally, the foliage of all the lungworts, which remains tidy throughout the summer, acts as an excellent weed cover.

In the shadier parts of the border *Hepatica triloba* with its leathery, ivy like leaves and true blue flowers, together with primulas and polyanthus will all make

pools of color in April and May. The golden flower of *Alyssum saxatile flore pleno* will shine even more brightly in association with the white flowers of the perennial candytuft *Iberis sempervirens* 'Snowflake', in sunny spots at the edge of the border.

Heucheras and heucherellas will enliven the early summer scene with their spikes of brilliant coral and clear pink miniature bells. The latter is an interesting hybrid between heuchera and tiarella, the foam flower, which is useful both for its decorative value at this time and as an evergreen carpeting plant later in the season. All these will do well in partial shade.

A complete contrast both in flowers and its ferny foliage is *Dicentra spectabilis,* the lyre flower, better known as bleeding heart. This plant prefers partial shade and blooms in late spring, at the same time as the graceful Solomon's seal, *Polygonatum multiflorum,* with its hanging bells of greenish white.

To provide color continuity from late summer onwards there are, in addition to the indispensable fall or perennial aster, various other perennial and bulbous plants. The gray leaved *Anaphalis triplinervis* is one of these. Its papery 'everlasting' white star like flowers, which first appear in July, will still be immaculate in October. The Japanese anemone, *Anemone hupehensis,* of which there are now many lovely named varieties, will start to put up clusters of chalice like blossoms from early August until the first heavy frosts arrive. The single forms, both pink and white, are still firm favorites, but if you are looking for something out of the ordinary you might like to try 'Margarete', a double pink, with rows of ruff like petals. 'Prince Henry', sometimes listed as 'Profusion', is one of the most striking singles, its color

1 Pyrethrum 'Eileen May Robinson' flowers in May.
2 Gaillardia 'Wirral Flame' is one of the most reliable cultivars.
3 Ligularia, with its large, rather floppy leaves, is a dramatic plant for a moist spot or the back of a border.
4 Thalictrum aquilegifolium, a soft and dainty flowering plant for the border, blooms in late summer and early autumn.

much richer than those of the other pinks.

In sheltered bays in the border from August onwards two closely allied South African bulbous plants will make a welcome splash of color. The blue African lily, *Agapanthus campanulatus,* has drumstick heads of powder blue flowers, while those of *Nerine bowdenii* are similar, but less tightly packed with pink florets. 'Fenwick's Variety', an attractive pink, is the best form for out of doors. These 2 plants do not tolerate temperatures much below 25°F.

And so the year goes by in the herbaceous border, with the first Christmas roses plumping up their buds as the last lingering flowers of the border chrysanthemums shrivel and fade. In the well-planned perennial border in mild climates there need never be a dull moment.

Winter work Apart from the periodic division, replanting and occasional replanning of the border, winter maintenance will consist mainly of tidying up and light forking between the plants. There are two schools of thought where the former operation is concerned. Some gardeners prefer to leave the tidying of the border until spring — the dead leaves and stems, they claim, protect the crowns of the plants in severe weather. Others, who cannot stand the sight of so much dead untidy vegetation, cut down the dead stems at the earliest opportunity.

There is much to be said for the former point of view, but a lot will depend on how the border is located. If it is in full view of the house windows, the sooner it is made shipshape the better. Only a very small number of popular herbaceous perennials are delicate enough to suffer irreparable damage, even in the severest winter. Plants such as eremurus and *Lobelia fulgens,* which may be damaged by frosts, can be protected by covering their crowns with a coarse mulch.

Where the border is more remotely situated, clearing up operations can take their place among garden tasks that make their demands during the winter months.

Others uses of herbaceous plants Perennials have become so closely associated in our minds with the herbaceous border that we tend to overlook their many other uses in the garden. For example, bedding schemes employing perennials can be just as attractive as those in which the more orthodox hardy and half hardy annuals are used. What is more important, management and upkeep will be simplified and costs will be less where these versatile plants are utilized.

Perennials as bedding plants For bedding purposes, it will be necessary to choose perennials with a relatively long flowering season and/or attractive foliage, plus a solid and compact habit of growth. Among those fulfilling such requirements

are *Brunnera macrophylla* (syn. *Anchusa myosotidiflora*), the so-called giant forget-me-not, *Anemone hupehensis,* the Japanese anemone, *Armeria maritima,* thrift, the medium and dwarf fall or perennial aster and dwarf delphiniums, for example *Delphinium chinensis.* The two last named, in common with a number of other perennials, have the added advantage of being easy to grow from seed.

Segregation of groups and species Another good way of making the best use of certain groups and species is to grow them in beds restricted to the one type of perennial. By growing them in this way, it is easy to make satisfactory provision for their special requirements in the way of feeding, staking, tying and general cultivation.

This works well for herbaceous plants such as lupin, iris, peonies, oriental poppies and the taller delphiniums. A further point in favor of this method is that it avoids the bare patches that tend to appear in the border when such early flowering perennials form part of the general scheme.

Other herbaceous perennials that will benefit from this method of culture are the fall or perennial aster. Where sufficient space is available, a representative collection, grown in a bed or border devoted to them would make a far greater impact than they would dotted about in groups in

Geranium pratense is a floriferous plant which makes good full clumps quickly.

the mixed border.

Waterside planting Although the great majority of perennials will thrive in a wide range of garden soils and situations, there are some that prefer shade and moisture, conditions that cannot always be easily provided in the herbaceous border. These make excellent plants for the waterside — by the banks of streams or artificial watercourses or at the edge of a garden pool.

Primulas, astilbes, *Iris sibirica* and *Iris kaempferi*, marsh marigold or cowslip (*Caltha palustris*) and the globe flower (*Trollius* species) are just a few plants that will grow better in damp, shady positions.

Cut flowers Satisfying the demands for flowers for the house in summer, when they fade so quickly, sometimes results in the display in the border being spoiled by too lavish cutting. A satisfactory way of avoiding this is to grow perennials especially for the purpose, either in rows in the vegetable garden or bordering the vegetable plot. For this, it is only common sense to choose those that will not only cut and last well, but will also need minimum attention where staking and tying are concerned. The list (*right*) is representative, but far from exhaustive.

It should be obvious, from the foregoing, that the uses of perennials are many and varied. We are doing ourselves a great disservice if we restrict them solely to the herbaceous border.

A selection of herbaceous plants

Name	Height in feet	Color	Season
Acanthus	4—5	lilac-pink	July—Aug
Achillea spp & vars	1—4	white, yellow	June—Aug
Alchemilla	1—1½	yellow-green	June—July
Anaphalis	1—2	white	July—Sept
Aquilegia hybs	1—3	various	May—June
Armeria	1	pinks	June—July
Artemisia	3—5	gray foliage	Aug—Sept
Aster spp & vars	1—5	various	Aug—Oct
Astrantia	2—3	green-pink	June
Bergenia	1—1½	pinks, white	March—April
Campanula	1—4	blues, white	June—Aug
Centaurea	2—5	blues, yellow	July—Sept
Cimicifuga	2—4	creamy-white	June—Sept
Coreopsis	2—3	golden-yellow	May—Oct
Corydalis	1	yellow	June—July
Delphinium	3—8	blues, mauves	May—June
Dianthus	½—1½	various	April—May
Dicentra	1—2	pink	March—April
Doronicum	1—2½	yellow	Aug—Sept
Echinacea	2—3	purple-red	July—Aug
Echinops	2—5	steely blue	June—Sept
Erigeron hybs	1—2	blue, pink	July—Aug
Eryngium	2—4	glaucous blue	April—June
Euphorbia	1—3	yellow	July—Aug
Gaillardia hybs	2	yellow, orange	June—July
Galega	2—4	mauve	July—Aug
Gentiana	1—2	blues	June—Aug
Geranium	1—2½	pinks, mauves	July—Sept
Helenium	3—5	yellows, copper	July—Sept
Hemerocallis	2—3	yellow, orange	May—Aug
Heuchera hybs	1—2½	pinks, reds	May—June
Iris	1—5	various	July—Sept
Kniphofia	1½—4	yellow, orange	June
Lupin hybs	2—4	various	June—Sept
Lythrum	2—4	purple-red	July—Sept
Lysimachia	2—4	yellow, white	July—Sept
Macleaya	5—8	apricot pink	July
Malva	2—4	mauves, pinks	June—Aug
Monarda	2—4	various	May—Sept
Nepeta	1—2	blue	May—June
Peony spp & hybs	2—4	pink, red, white	July—Sept
Phlox	2—4	various	May—June
Pyrethrum	1—3	various	June—Sept
Salvia spp	2—5	mauves	June—Aug
Sidalcea hybs	2½—5	pinks	July—Oct
Verbascum	3—8	yellow, pink	July—Oct
Veronica spp & vars	1—3	blues, mauves	

Perennials for cutting

Name	Height in feet	Color	Season
Acanthus mollis	4—5	lilac-pink	July—Aug
Achillea 'Moonshine'	2	sulphur-yellow	June—July
Alchemilla mollis	1—1½	yellowish-green	June—July
Anaphalis triplinervis	¾	white 'everlasting'	July—Aug
Aquilegia hybrids	up to 3	various	May—June
Aster (perennial)	up to 5	white, pinks, purples	Aug—Oct
Astrantia	2—3	greenish-white, pink	June
Coreopsis grandiflora	2—3	golden-yellow	June—Sept
Dianthus	½—1	various	May—June
Heuchera spp & varieties	2	pinks, reds	June—July
Iris germanica	up to 3	various	May—June
Phlox decussata	up to 3	various	July—Sept
Pyrethrum varieties	2	various	May—June
Trollius	2	yellow, gold	May—June

Acanthus (ak-an-thus)

From the Greek *akanthos*, a spine *(Acanthaceae)*. Bear's breech. Handsome hardy perennials known to the Greeks and Romans, who used the leaf form of *Acanthus mollis* for the decoration of the Corinthian column.

Species cultivated *A. caroli-alexandri*, 1—1½ feet, white or rose flowers in July. *A. longifolius*, up to 3—4 feet, purple flowers in June. *A. mollis*, the best known species, 3—4 feet, with white, pink or mauve flowers and great bold leaves 2 feet long; vars. *latifolius* with wider leaves and white flowers, *nigrum*, with glossy, spineless leaves and lilac-white flowers. *A. spinosus*, 4 feet, very prickly deeply divided leaves, a handsome plant with purple, green and white flowers in July and August.

Cultivation Excellent as specimen plants where their form and character can be appreciated, acanthus stand erect without support. Tenacious because of their stout roots, they can withstand both drought and wind. The foliage of the young plants is less pointed and not as deeply cut as that of mature plants, and root cuttings taken from young plants will produce plants of less jagged leaf shape. Grow them in well drained loam, preferably, but not necessarily, in a sunny position. Propagate by seed sown in mild spring warmth, or by root cuttings in winter or spring, or division in autumn or spring. Hardy to 15°F.

Achillea (ak-ill-e-a)

Name after Achilles, who is said to have used it as a treatment for his wounds *(Compositae)*. Yarrow, milfoil. Hardy perennials, for the border or border rock garden.

1 Kniphofia 'Royal Standard', the Red Hot Poker, is just one of the many beautiful and unusual kinds of perennials.
2 Acanthus spinosus is the Bear's Breech, used decoratively by the early Greeks and Romans.
3 Achillea filipendulina 'Gold Plate' is effectively used in dried arrangements.

Species cultivated: Border *A. filipendulina*, large, plate like heads of yellow flowers in summer; cultivars include 'Gold Plate', 4—5 feet, 'Flowers of Sulphur', 2½ feet, soft sulphur yellow flowers and powdered leaves, and 'Canary Bird', 1½—2 feet. *A. millefolium*, yarrow or milfoil; cultivars are 'Cerise Queen', 2 feet, with rose-cerise flowers in July in a loose head, 'Crimson Beauty', 2½ feet, and 'Fire King', 2—2½ feet (probably the best). *A. ptarmica* (sneezewort), 2 feet, white flowered, has several good cultivars of which 'The Pearl', 2½ feet, with small, tightly double flowers is the best. *A. sibirica*, 1½ feet, white flowers; 'Perry's White', 2—3 feet, is a fine variety.

Rock Garden *A. ageratifolia*, 4 inches, gray-white leaves and white flowers. *A. chrysocoma*, mats of gray leaves, flowers yellow on 4—6 inch stems. *A. huteri*, silvery tufts, short stemmed white flowers. *A.* 'King Edward' (syn. *A. × lewsii*) 4 inches, gray-green mats, buff-yellow flowers all summer. *A. portae*, 4 inches, gray leaves, white flowers. *A. prichardii* 4 inches, gray mats, white flowers. *A. rupestris*, 4—6 inches, foliage creeping, sprays of white flowers, May. *A. tommentosa*, 9 inches, leaves grey, flowers golden-yellow; needs protection from winter dampness; var. *aurea* flowers deeper yellow.

Cultivation Achilleas flourish in almost any soil, provided it is not very acid or water logged, and revel in sunshine. They prefer lime but are quite tolerant of acid conditions. They have tiny or double daisy like flowers collected in loose clusters or flat heads and bloom in summer. Foliage is fern like, stems stiff and unbreakable and the fragrance somewhat pungent. Some varieties are recommended for winter arrangements of dried flowers, the best being *A. filipendula*, 'Gold Plate', and if the heads are stored in powdered alum until quite dry, they last well and retain all their color. Plant in autumn or spring or divide the plants at this time. Sow seed ¼ inch deep in early summer. Border kinds should be lifted and divided every three or four years and the shoots cut down in winter.

Alchemilla (al-kem-il-a)

From *alkemelych*, an Arabic word, indicating the plant's use in alchemy *(Rosaceae)*. Lady's mantle. Hardy herbaceous low growing plants suitable for use on rock

gardens or at the fronts of borders. The flowers are in clusters, in shades of green or yellow, in July.

Species cultivated *A. alpina,* 6 inches, handsome foliage, gray-green above, silvery below, flowers pale greenish-yellow. When grown on the rock garden, it is best planted in crevices between rocks. *A. mollis,* 12 inches, attractive, with kidney shaped, wavy edged, softly hairy leaves and greenish-yellow flowers, good for cutting. Contrasts well when grown in association with *Campanula poscharskyana.* Inclined to be invasive when established, but well worth growing, especially as ground cover in shady or semi shady places, such as under trees.

Cultivation Drainage must not be impaired for alchemillas to thrive well; otherwise any ordinary garden soil suits

Alchemilla mollis, Lady's Mantle, is a good, delicately flowered cover for shady situations.

them. They are best transplanted in autumn or spring. As they are spreading plants, division is a simple means of propagation and they set seed freely. This may be collected with the aid of polythene bags, placed over the faded flower heads, and sown in spring.

Alternanthera (al-tern-an-the-ra)

Alluding to the fact that alternate anthers are usually infertile *(Amaranthaceae).* Used in the main for foliage effect, these half hardy shrubby perennials have brightly colored foliage. The flowers are insignificant and are not usually allowed to develop.

Species cultivated *A. amoena,* 3 inches, leaves, green veined with orange-red blotches; vars. *amabilis* (leaves orange-scarlet), *rosea* and *spectabilis. A. bettickiana,* 3—4 inches, leaves blotched with shades of yellow and red. Has given rise to most popularly grown forms: *aurea,* golden yellow leaves; *magnifica,* leaves similar to, though brighter than the species; *paronychioides,* leaves basically orange-red with olive green tints, red tips on young foliage; *spathulata,* 6—8 inches, stems and leaves red, underneath bronzy overtones. *A. versicolor,* 3—4 inches, leaves coppery red.

Cultivation An ordinary garden soil is suitable and a sunny position should be chosen. Plant 2 inches apart for massed effect. Set the plants out in May and lift in September after the first frost, when they are trimmed to 3—4 inches. Store for winter on the dry side in a temperature of 50—55°F. Propagate by division of stored plants in spring, rooted offsets being grown on. Cuttings can be taken in August, rooted with heat in winter and potted in spring.

Althaea (al-the-a)

Referring to its medicinal use, from the Greek *althaea,* to cure *(Malvaceae).* A genus of easily grown plants comprising annuals, biennials and perennials.

Biennial species cultivated *A. ficifolia* (fig-leaved or Antwerp hollyhock), to 6 feet, single or double flowers in spikes of mostly yellow, June. *A. rosea,* hollyhock, erect growing, to 9 feet or sometimes a good deal more. Tall spikes of single or double flowers, sometimes 3 inches or more across, in shades of red, pink, yellow and white, July. This is strictly a perennial but is often treated as a biennial.

Perennial species cultivated *A. cannabina,* 5—6 feet, rose flowers, June; var. *narbonensis,* red flowers. *A. officinalis* (marsh mallow), 4 feet, blush colored flowers, July.

Cultivars of hollyhocks 'Charter's Improved', fully double flowers, mixed colors. 'Apple Blossom', apple-bossom pink. 'Carmine Rose', double cherry-red flowers; and other separate colors. 'Allegheny Mammoth', mixed colors, single and semi-double. 'Begonia Flowered', fringed petals with central rosette, mixed. Annual hollyhock: 'Triumph Supreme', to 4 feet, compact growing.

Cultivation Hollyhocks will succeed in most soils, but prefer the heavier kinds, especially if they are fertilized. They need plenty of water in dry periods and should be firmly staked with stout stakes 7 feet or more long, driven well into the ground, to prevent wind damage, particularly in exposed gardens. Stems should be cut down to within about 6 inches of the ground after flowering is over.

Anaphalis (an-af-a-lis)

Said to be an old Greek name for a similar plant *(Compositae).* Hardy perennials with white woolly foliage and flowers which can be cut before maturity and dried for use as 'everlastings', sometimes being dyed.

Species cultivated *A. margaritacea* (pearly everlasting), 1 foot, white throughout, flowering June—August. *A. nubigena*, 6—9 inches, silvery white foliage, flowers white, summer. *A. triplinervis*, 12—18 inches, soft woolly silver foliage, pearly-white flowers, June—August. *A. yedoensis*, 2 feet, leaves grey above, white below, flowers white, summer.

Cultivation Anaphalis are suitable for the rock garden or for borders, according to size. An ordinary garden soil and a sunny position suits them. They do well on alkaline soils. Plant in autumn or spring. Established plants may be increased by division at the same seasons. New plants may also be raised from seed sown outside in April.

Anchusa (an-chu-sa)

The name originates from the Greek *anchousa*, a cosmetic paint *(Boraginaceae)*. Alkanet, bugloss. Cultivated species are usually perennials or biennials, noteworthy for their blue flowers. The plant long known as *Anchusa myosotidiflora* is now correctly known as *Brunnera macrophylla*.

Biennial species cultivated *A. capensis*, 18 inches, flowers in panicles at tips of stems, July. *A. officinalis*, 1—2 feet, flowers sometimes purple in double spikes, May; var. *incarnata*, flowers pale pink.

Perennial species cultivated *A. azurea* (syn. *A. italica*), 3—5 feet, bright blue flowers summer. *A. barrelieri*, 2 feet, flowers, blue and white, yellow throats, May. *A. caespitosa* (syn. *A. angustissima*), 12—15 inches, tufted plant with gentian blue flowers from May to July, rock garden or alpine house. *A. sempervirens*, 1½—2 feet, rich blue flowers, May; var. *variegata*, foliage cream and green.

Cultivars *A. azurea* — 'Dropmore', 'Loddon Royalist', 'Morning Glory', 'Opal', 'Pride of Dover', 'Suttons Bright Blue', 'Suttons Royal Blue' *A. capenis* — 'Blue Bird'.

Cultivation Sunny borders in ordinary soil. Plant in autumn or spring. Perennials may be raised from seed, from root cuttings taken in February, or by dividing established plants in October. Biennials are raised from seed sown in April.

Aquilegia (ak-wil-e-je-a)

The flower form resembles an eagle's claw, hence the probable origin of this name from *aquila* the Latin for eagle *(Ranunculaceae)*. Columbine. Hardy herbaceous perennials for the herbaceous border and rock garden. The flowers and leaves are very dainty. Unfortunately they are inclined to be short lived in heavy wet soils, but they are easily increased by seed. The flowers appear in May and June in a wide range of colors from yellows and creams to blues and reds and purples. The garden hybrids have been raised from various

species, e.g. the long spurred hybrids from *A. longissima*. 'Mrs Scott Elliott's' is a well-known strain, and more recently there are the McKana Giant hybrids, with larger flowers and long spurs.

Species cultivated *A. alpina*, 1 foot, flowers blue, white center. *A. atrata*, 9 inches, purple-red flowers. *A. bertolonii*, 6 inches, flowers deep violet-blue. *A. caerulea*, 1½—2½ feet, flowers pale blue and white; various named forms, such as 'Blue King', 'Crimson Star', *candidissima* ('Snow Queen'), pure white, *cuprea* ('Copper Queen') coppery, 'Dragon Fly' a dwarf strain in various colors. *A. canadensis*, 1½ feet, pale yellow. *A. chrysantha*, 2—4 feet, golden-yellow. *A. clematiflora hybrida*, 1½ feet, spurless flowers in pink and blue shades. *A. discolor*, 3 inches, blue and white flowers. *A. flabellata*, 9 inches, white, tinged pink, var. *nana alba*, 6 inches, flowers white. *A. formosa*, 1½ feet, yellow or yellow and red flowers; var. *truncata*, smaller flowers. *A. fragrans*, 1½—2 feet, white or purple fragrant; needs a sunny sheltered position. *A. glandulosa*, 1 foot, lilac and white flowers. *A. helenae*, 1½ feet, blue and white. *A. longissima*, 2 feet, long spurred yellow flowers. *A. skinneri*, 2 feet, crimson flowers. *A. viridiflora*, 9 inches, green and brown, fragrant. *A. vulgaris*, the common columbine, 1½—2½ feet, various colors and forms including the very double *flore pleno*.

Cultivation The requirements are sun or partial shade and a loamy soil enriched with leafmold and not too heavy or dry. Dwarf species, grown on the rock garden, need well drained soil and full sun. Plants do well on slightly alkaline soils. Seed is sown in May or June in the open, in August in a frame or the plants may be divided in spring or autumn.

Armeria (ar-meer-e-a)

This genus has retained the old Latin name for pink although it is not related to the true pink, a species of dianthus *(Plumbaginaceae)*. Perennials mainly for the rock garden though the taller kinds are sometimes used at the front of the herbaceous border. They all need well drained, sunny positions and grow well in seaside gardens; the common thrift, in fact, grows wild in extensive colonies on cliffs by the sea.

Species cultivated *A. caespitosa*, 2 inches, a true alpine so it must have good drainage, flowers pale lilac in early summer, a good plant for the alpine house; vars. *alba*, flowers white; *rubra*, ruby red. *A. corsica*, 6 inches, brick red. *A. maritima*, the common thrift or sea pink, 6 inches, flowers pink in early summer.

1 Althaea rosea, the well-known Hollyhock, one of the tallest of hardy perennials, is available in a wide range of colors.
2 Anaphalis nubigena is an everlasting flower with silvery white foliage.

There are good cultivars of this species such as *laucheana,* 9 inches, bright red flowers; *nana alba,* with large, white flowers in May and June; 'Merlin', rich pink, and 'Vindictive', masses of reddish-pink flowers. *A. pseudoarmeria,* sea pink, thrift, 1 foot, a handsome plant for the herbaceous border; the bright rose colored flowers appear in June. The cultivar 'Bees Ruby' was developed from this species and is taller, at 2 feet, and bears rounded heads of deep rose flowers in early summer. *A. splendens,* 3—4 inches, pale pink, summer.

Cultivation Any good, sandy loam suits these plants which must have well-drained positions either in the herbaceous border or on the rock garden. Propagate by division of roots in autumn or spring when they should also be planted. Seeds can be sown in spring in sandy soil.

Artemisia (ar-tem-ees-e-a)

Named after Artemis the Greek goddess *(Compositae).* A large genus, widely distributed over the world, of shrubs, subshrubs, herbaceous perennials and annuals, grown mainly for their dainty, aromatic foliage which is very finely cut in some species. The genus shows a great diversity of habit and leaf shape: the flowers are very small and are seldom of much account, though they are often borne in large panicles or plumes. The tarragon herb used for flavorings and vinegar is a member of this family. Most of the artemisias are sun lovers, but *A. lactiflora,* with its sprays of creamy white flowers, will grow in semishade and is a useful plant for the herbaceous border.

Annual species cultivated *A. sacrorum viridis,* summer fire, 4 feet, strictly a subshrub but grown as an annual.

Herbaceous and sub-shrubs *A. absinthium,* wormwood, 1½ feet, flowers yellow, summer. There is a good form, 'Lambrook Silver' useful for the gray border. *A. baumgartenii,* 9 inches, silvery leaves, yellow flowers, late summer. *A. canescens,* 1 foot, makes a dome of silvery leaves and is suitable for the rock garden. *A. dracunculus,* tarragon, 2 feet, whitish-green. *A. filifolia,* dwarf carpeting plant with bright silvery foliage. *A. glacialis,* 3—6 inches, silvery leaves, yellow flowerheads. A plant for a scree in the rock garden or for the alpine house. *A. gnaphalodes,* 2 feet, foliage gray-white. *A. lactiflora,* 4 feet, creamy white flowers in plumes, late summer. *A. lanata,* 4—6 inches, silvery leaves, yellow flowers.

Rock Garden *A. ludoviciana,* 3 feet, silvery leaves, yellow flowers, summer. *A. maritima,* sea wormwood, 1—1½ feet, silvery-white leaves, yellowish to reddish flowers, summer. *A. nutans,* 1½—2 feet, finely cut silver-gray leaves. *A. pedemontana,* 6 inches, silvery leaves, rock garden. *A. pontica,* 1—2 feet, gray foliage, whitish-yellow flowers, late summer. *A. stelleriana,* 2—3 feet, silvery leaves, yellow flowers. *A. purshiana,* 2½ feet, white leaves, used as a foliage plant. *A. vulgaris,*

1 *Anchusa azurea is a delicate border plant.*
2 *Armeria pseudoarmeria is the summer blooming Sea Pink.*
3 *Dainty Aquilegia is the well loved Columbine.*

mugwort, 2—4 feet, purplish or yellow flowers, autumn. This species spreads rapidly becoming a weed difficult to control.

Shrubs *A. abrotanum,* 3—4 feet, the well-known old man or southernwood, fragrant, gray, filigree foliage. *A. arborescens,* 3 feet, silvery foliage retained throughout the year. The flowers of both these shrubs, when produced, are insignificant. They are grown for their foliage.

Cultivation Plant in autumn or spring in sunny borders in ordinary soil. Propagate shrubby species by summer cuttings and herbaceous by cuttings or division. Seeds may be sown in spring of annual and herbaceous species.

Aster (as-ter)

From the Greek *aster,* star, describing the flower shape *(Compositae).* Fall or perennial aster, sometimes known as Michaelmas daisy. Among the most useful herbaceous perennials, most of the asters flower in late summer right into the autumn and are extremely hardy and easy to grow. They increase so rapidly, in fact, that many of them have to be lifted and divided about every second year. There are a great

1 Artemisia gnaphalodes with its whitish leaves makes a good border plant.
2 and 3 Pink 'Beechwood' is a summer-flowering Aster alpinus.

many cultivars suitable for the back of the herbaceous border, growing to about 6 feet in height, derived from *A. novi-belgii* and *A. novae-angliae* but there are also shorter, bushier cultivars, up to 3 feet in height that have been raised from *A. amellus* and *A. frikhartii.* These shorter varieties are also earlier flowering than the taller kinds. The really dwarf cultivars, 9—15 inches tall, are excellent plants for the front of a border, as they are compact and very free flowering.

There are asters, too, for the rock garden, such as *A. subcaeruleus,* which flowers in June; the bright violet-blue flowers are produced on 9 inch stems and stand up above the foliage which makes small clumps as it spreads.

The two groups, *A. novi-belgii* and *A. novae-angliae* are very similar, but the foliage in the *novi-belgii* group is smooth, whereas that of *novae-angliae* is downy.

A great deal of hybridizing has been carried out with Fall asters or Michaelmas

daisies, the largest variations are to be seen in the *novi-belgii* group where the colors range from white, pinks, mauves, to deep rose-pink and purple. There are double and single flowers, and some of the varieties are short and bushy, more like the *amellus* group. In the *nova-angliae* group the colors are confined to deep pinks and purples and the flowers have an unfortunate habit of closing at sundown.

Species cultivated *A. acris,* 3 feet, masses of lavender-blue flowers in midsummer. *A. alpinus,* 6 inches, purple flowers in midsummer; 'Beechwood' is a fine cultivar. *A. amellus,* 2 feet, purple flowers in midsummer. *A. cordifolius,* 2 feet, mauve flowers on arching stems in summer. *A. ericoides,* 2—3 feet, abundant white flowers in autumn, angular branching habit: 'Perfection', 4 feet, white and 'Ring-dove', 4 feet, rosy mauve, are two cultivars. *A. farreri,* 1½ feet, flowers long rayed, violet-blue in summer. *A.* × *frikartii,* 3 feet, flowers lavender-blue, in midsummer; 'Wonder of Staff', lavender-blue, is a popular cultivar. *A. lino-syris,* goldilocks, 1½ feet, a native with showy golden-yellow flowers in late summer. *A. novae-angliae,* 5—6 feet, autumn-flowering, purple flowers. *A. novi-belgii,* 4 feet, blue flowers in autumn. *A. pappei,* 1 foot, bright blue flowers throughout summer and early autumn. Not reliably hardy except in milder places. *A. subcaeruleus,* 9 inches, violet-blue flowers on 9 inch stems above the foliage; 'Wendy', 1½ feet, pale blue with orange center, a fine cultivar. *A. thomsonii,* 15 inches, pale blue, a parent, with *A. amellus,* of the hybrid *A.* × *frikartii. A. tradescantii,* 4 feet, white flowers in autumn. *A. yunnanensis,* 1 foot, lilac-blue flowers in summer; 'Napsbury' has larger flowers of heliotrope-blue.

Cultivars Named cultivars of the major groups are numerous and new ones seem to appear each year and it is worth visiting a nursery or consulting an up to date

1 *The Astilbe hybrid 'White Queen' is an excellent plant for moist soils, bog gardens and the sides of streams or ponds.*
2 *The unspectacular flowers of Astrantia major repay close examination.*

catalogue before ordering plants. Among the best are the following:
Amellus 'Blue King', 2½ feet, bright blue. 'King George', 2½ feet, bright blue; an old favorite. 'Sonia', 2 feet, clear pink.
Novae-angliae 'Barr's Pink', 4 feet, 'Harrington's Pink', 4½ feet, clear pink, both old varieties. 'Lye End Beauty', 4 feet, pale plum and 'September Glow', 5 feet, ruby, are both newer varieties.
Novi-belgii 'Apple Blossom', 3 feet, cream, overlaid pink. 'Blue Radiance', 3 feet, large flowers, soft blue. 'Crimson Brocade', 3 feet, bright red, double. 'Little Pink Boy', 2 feet, deep pink. 'Marie Ballard', 3 feet, mid blue, large fully double. 'My Smokey', 6 feet, deep mulberry, vigorous. 'Orlando', 3½ feet, clear pink, single. 'Peerless', 4 feet, soft heliotrope, semi double. 'Sailing Light', 3 feet, deep rose. 'Sweet Seventeen', 4 feet, lavender-pink, fully double. 'The Cardinal', 5 feet, rose-red. 'The Rector', 3½ feet, claret. 'White Lady', 5—6 feet, pure white. 'Winston Churchill', 2½ feet, ruby-crimson.
Dwarf 'Audrey', 15 inches, large, pale blue. 'Lilac Time', 1 foot, soft lilac. 'Pink Lace', 15 inches, double pink. 'Professor A. Kippenburg', 15 inches, light blue, semi-double. 'Snow Cushion', 10 inches, white. 'Victor', 9 inches, light blue.
Cultivation Their cultivation is simple: plant in the autumn or spring except the *amellus* group which dislikes autumn planting and so must be planted and divided in the spring. They like a sunny position but will tolerate a little shade, and though they will repay good cultivation they are not fussy about soil. They are readily increased by division. Attacks by

powdery mildew often whiten the leaves and make them unsightly.

Astilbe (as-til-be)

Many of the older species had colorless flowers which may be the origin of the name, from the Greek *a,* no, *stilbe, rightness (Saxifragaceae).* A small genus of herbaceous perennials with feathery plumes composed of myriads of minute flowers in white, many in shades of pink and deep crimson. They are delightful waterside plants but they will grow in the herbaceous border if given a good, rich, moist soil. They will grow well in partial shade and there are dwarf species suitable for the rock garden.

Species cultivated *A. chinensis pumila,* 1 foot, rose-lilac flowers in late summer. *A. crispa,* 6 inches, salmon-pink flowers, summer. *A. davidii,* 4—5 feet, rose pink flowers in late summer. *A. japonica,* 2 feet, white flowers in spring. *A. simplicifolia erecta,* 9 inches, pink flowers in arching sprays in summer. *A. thunbergii,* 1—2 feet, white flowers in May.

Cultivars 'Amethyst', 3 feet, lilac-purple. 'Cattleya', 3 feet, orchid-pink. 'Fanal', 2 feet, garnet red. 'Feuer', crimson with deep crimson foliage. 'Granat', 3 feet, rose-crimson. 'Professor Van der Weilan', 3 feet white. 'Red Sentinel', 2 feet, brick red. 'Rhineland', 2½ feet, rich rose pink. 'Venus', 3 feet, deep pink. 'White Queen', 2½ feet. All these are known as *A.* × *arendsii* hybrids and are of complex parentage. Others will be found in nurserymen's lists.

Cultivation Plant in autumn or spring and water well in dry weather. Propagate by division or seeds. Astilbes may also be grown as early flowering greenhouse plants. They should be potted in the early autumn in a compost of loam, leaf mold and sand. Pots should be kept plunged outdoors until December when they may be brought into the greenhouse and forced into early

flower at a temperature of 55—60°F. After flowering is over the plants should be hardened off, after which they may be planted outdoors again in May.

Astrantia (as-tran-te-a)
Starlike flowers, hence the name from the Greek *aster*, a star *(Umbelliferae)*. Masterwort. Summer flowering perennials with fascinating papery looking flowers in shades of green, white and pink. The actual flowers are insignificant but they are surrounded by parchment like bracts that give them color. They make excellent and unusual cut flowers.

Species cultivated *A. biebersteinii*, 2 feet, flowers light lilac. *A. carinthiaca*, 1—2 feet, very similar to *A. major* with which it is often confused, flowers fragrant of marzipan. *A. carniolica*, 2 feet, white or bluish-pink flowers; var. *rubra*, reddish. *A. major*, 2 feet, pink, suffused with green. *A. maxima*, 2 feet, pink flowers, leaves bright green. *A. minor*, 9 inches, pale purple flowers, tinted green.

Cultivation Plant astrantias in the autumn or spring in ordinary soil in a shady position in the border or woodland garden. They will grow in more open positions provided they are not hot and dry. Propagate by division at planting time or grow from seeds sown in sandy loam in April in a cold frame.

Bellis (bel-lis)
From the Latin *bellus*, pretty, handsome *(Compositae)*. The double daisy, a garden variety of one of our commonest wild plants, was cultivated in Elizabethan gardens side by side with double forms of the native buttercup. The original name was 'day's eye' as the little plant opened or closed according to the light.

Species cultivated *B. perennis*, the common daisy, 3—6 inches, white, April onwards. A plant widely distributed and if allowed to set seed may become a weed in

1 Bellis perennis florepleno, the Double Daisy, is a useful carpeting plant for spring. 2 Bergenia cordifolia flowers in March, one of the earliest perennials to bloom.

lawns. A weed, but the parent of many cultivated forms. *B. rotundifolia caerulescens*, 3 inches, a tiny white daisy tinted with pale blue, a native of Algeria. *B. sylvestris*, 4—6 inches, daisies with yellow discs and bright red surrounding florets, Mediterranean area.

Cultivated double daisies include many named forms of the double daisy, *Bellis perennis flore pleno*. At least a dozen forms or strains are obtainable with more or less crimson in their coloring and varying also in size and doubling of the flowers and petal formation. In most of these the golden 'eye' is eliminated. All grow about 6 inches tall and their neatness and ability to produce large quantities of flowers makes them most useful in spring bedding schemes.

Cultivation The double forms of *B. perennis* are very hardy herbaceous perennials which do not demand special soil or garden location. They are raised from seed sown in July or August, or old plants may be divided in June, the pieces quickly making new plants if placed in a shaded bed or prepared soil. Often grown as a biennial.

Both *B. rotundifolia caerulescens* and *B. sylvestris* are suitable for the rock garden where they must have a sheltered position and a free draining soil. The former may need winter protection.

Bergenia (ber-gen-i-a)
Named for Karl August von Bergen, 1704-60, German botanist *(Saxifragaceae)*. These hardy perennial herbaceous plants with large evergreen leaves were at one time listed in catalogs as saxifrage or *megasea*. The flowers which come in early spring are showy in white, pink or

red-purple, borne in large heads on long stems. The large leathery, glossy leaves are also decorative, especially as in some kinds the foliage is suffused with reddish color in winter.

Species cultivated *B. cordifolia*, 1 foot, pink, spring; var. *purpurea*, flowers purplish-pink. *B. crassifolia*, 1 foot, pink, spring. *B. delavayi*, 9 inches, leaves turn crimson in winter, flowers purplish-rose, March, *B. ligulata*, 1 foot, white or pink, January or February onwards, *B. × schmidtii*, 1 foot, flowers pink spring. *B. stracheyi*, 1 foot, pink, April.

Cultivars 'Ballawley Hybrid', 1½ feet, crimson flowers, dark purplish leaves in winter. 'Delbees', 1 foot, leaves turn red in winter, flowers rosy, March—April. 'Evening Glow', 15—18 inches, dark purple flowers, reddish-bronze foliage. 'Silberlich', ('Silver Light'), 1 foot, flowers white flushed pink, spring. Others are available and more are likely to be seen in cultivation as time goes on.

Cultivation These members of the saxifrage family are in no way difficult, thriving in any soil, in sun or shade. However, to get full color in the winter leaves, it will be necessary to give the bergenias full sun exposure; and under those conditions they will also produce their flowers somewhat earlier.

Callirrhoe (kal-ir-ho-ee)
Named after Callirhoe, one of the Greek goddesses *(Malvaceae)*. Poppy mallow. This North American genus has both annual and perennial species. The flowers are saucer shaped and of red hues, which are brilliant in sunshine. They need an open, sunny position.

Species cultivated *C. involucrata*, the Buffalo rose, 9 inches, flowers crimson, 2 inches across.

Cultivation *C. involucrata* likes a dry sunny spot, the hotter the better, but requires plenty of space to spread. Plant in

1 *Campanula trachelium*, the nettle-leaved *Bell Flower*, is an easy-to-grow autumn-flowering perennial that will flourish in the wild garden.

2 *Campanula fragilis* is a tufted form for the rock garden, which blooms in mid-summer.

November. Propagation is by seed sown out of doors in a nursery bed in April, the young plants transplanted later to their permanent position, or by cuttings of young growths taken in spring, and put in sandy compost in a cold frame.

Campanula (kam-pan-u-la)

From the Latin *campanula*, a little bell, hence the common name, Bellflower (*Campanulaceae*). A large genus of annuals, biennials and perennials for growing in the border, wild garden, rock garden and greenhouse; widely distributed over the Northern Hemisphere.

Border species cultivated *C. × burghaltii*, 2½ feet, large lavender bells, June and July, sandy soil. *C. carpatica*, 9 inches, edging plant, also rock garden, flowers blue, July and August, plant in the autumn before leaves die down, avoiding dormant season; cvs. 'Ditton Blue', 6 inches, indigo; 'Harvest Moon', violet-blue; 'Queen of Somerville', 15 inches, pale blue; *turbinata*, 6 inches, purple-blue; *turbinata pallida*, 6 inches, china blue; 'White Star', 1 foot. *C. grandis* (syn. *C. latiloba*), 3 feet, sturdy, rather stiff growth, flowers close set in spikes, open flat, blue, June and July, creeping root stock, lift every third year, grows in shade. *C. lactiflora*, the finest of the bellflowers, 4—5 feet, establishes well in good moist soil, stem erect, covered with foliage, branching to trusses of lavender flowers, July and August; vars. 'Loddon Anna', pale pink; 'Pritchard's Variety', deep blue; 'Pouffe', 1 foot, dwarf variety, light blue. *C. latifolia*, 2½ feet, blue, June to August, easy to grow, tolerates shade; vars. *alba*, white flowers; 'Brantwood', 4 feet, violet-purple; *macrantha*, deep violet flowers, this species sometimes attracts blackfly. *C. persicifolia*, the peach leaved bellflower, 2½—3 feet, best species to grow in the shade, sends out stolons and forms rosettes of leaves from which the wiry flowering stem grows, producing lavender flowers in June and July; vars. 'Fleur de Neige', 2 feet, semi double white; 'Snowdrift', single white; 'Telham Beauty', large, single, lavender-blue; 'Wedgwood Blue'; 'Wirral Belle', good double deep blue; also mixed 'Giant Hybrids'. *C. rotundifolia*, 3—4 inches, the English harebell and Scottish bluebell, well-known on alkaline and light soils, bears single nodding delicate flowers, July and August; var. *olympica*, 9 inches, lavender-blue, June to September. *C. sarmatica*, 1½ feet, spikes of pale blue flowers, July, grayish leaves.

Rock garden These are mainly dwarf species which require a gritty, well-drained soil and an open, sunny position, except where noted. All are summer flowering unless otherwise stated. *C. abietina*, 6 inches, violet. *C. alliariaefolia*, 2 feet, white. *C. arvatica*, 3 inches, deep violet, needs scree conditions; var. *alba*, white. *C. aucheri*, 4—6 inches, tufted habit, deep purple, early. *C. bellidifolia*, 4 inches, purplish blue. *C. calaminthifolia*, prostrate, gray leaves, soft blue flowers,

alpine house. *C. carpatica* (as border species). *C. cochlearifolia* (syn. *C. pusilla*), 3 inches, bright blue; vars. *alba*, white; 'Jewel' 4 inches, large, blue; *pallida*, pale blue. *C. elatines*, 6 inches, purple blue. *C. formaneckiana*, 15 inches, silver-gray leaves, pale blue or white flowers, monocarpic, best in the alpine house. *C. garganica*, 4 inches, blue, good wall plant; vars. *hirsuta*, light blue, hairy leaves, May onwards; 'W. H. Paine', dark blue, white centers. *C. hallii*, 4 inches, white. *C. herzegovinensis nana*, 1 inch, deep blue. *C. jenkinsae*, 6 inches, white. *C. kemmulariae*, 9—12 inches, mauve-blue. *C. linifolia*, 9 inches, purple. *C. nitida* (syn. *C. planiflora*), 9 inches, blue; var. *alba*, 6 inches, white. *C. portenschlagiana* (syn. *C. muralis*) 6 inches, trailing, purple, good wall plant. *C. poscharskyana*, 6 inches, powder blue, walls or banks; var. *lilacina*, lilac. *C. pulla*, 4 inches, violet, likes limy soil. *C. raddeana*, 1 foot, deep violet. *C. raineri*, 1 inch, china blue, scree plant. *C. sarmatica*, 9 inches, gray-blue leaves and flowers. *C. saxifraga*, 4 inches, deep purple. *C. speciosa*, 9 inches, purple blue. *C. stansfieldii*, 4 inches, violet. *C. tridentata*, 4—6 inches, deep blue. *C. valdensis*, 6 inches, gray leaves, violet flowers. *C. warleyensis*, 3 inches, blue, double.

Rock garden cultivars 'Birch Hybrid' (*C. portenschlagiana × C. poscharskyana*), 9 inches, purple blue; 'G. F. Wilson', 4 inches, violet-blue; 'Patience Bell', 3—4 inches, rich blue; 'Profusion', 4—5 inches, blue; 'R. B. Loder, semi double, mid-blue.

Wild garden The growth of these is too rampant for the border. *C. barbata*, 1 foot, clear pale blue flowers. *C. glomerata*, 1½ feet, head of closely packed deep purple flowers, June to August; vars. *acaulis*, 6 inches, violet-blue flowers; *dahurica*, 1 foot, violet; *superba*, 1 foot, purple. *C. rapunculoides*, 5 feet, drooping flowers, deep blue, spreads rapidly. *C. thyrsoides*, 1 foot, yellow bells in closely packed spike, summer, monocarpic. *C. trachelium*, 2 feet, purple-blue flowers on erect stems June and July.

Greenhouse *C. pyramidalis*, the chimney bellflower, a biennial, 4—5 feet, spectacular, covered with white or lavender flowers. *C. isophylla*, a trailing plant for hanging baskets or edge of greenhouse staging, lilac-blue flowers, summer; vars. *alba*, white flowers, *mayi*, woolly variegated leaves.

Biennial *C. medium*, Canterbury bell, 2½ feet, in shades of pink and blue, and also white forms; vars. *calycanthema*, the cup-and-saucer type; *flore pleno*, double, 3 feet, with white, blue or pink flowers. Cultivars include 'Dean's Hybrids' with single or double flowers.

Annual *C. ramosissima*, 6—12 inches, pale blue to violet, this is not often grown but may be used to fill gaps in borders. Sow seed in early April and thin seedlings to 4—6 inches apart.

Cultivation: Border Many of the border campanulas may be grown in partial shade; most like a well cultivated soil. Plant in spring or autumn. Stake tall species. They are propagated by seed sown in pans in very fine compost, with no covering of soil, put in a shaded frame. Prick out seedlings and harden them off before planting out. Propagate plants with creeping roots by division in autumn.

Rock garden Propagate these kinds by seed sown in March in frames, by division in spring, or by cuttings after flowering.

Wild garden Plant kinds suitable for the wild garden in spring or autumn, in sun or partial shade. Propagate by seed or division as for border kinds.

Biennial Seed of *C. pyramidalis* is sown in pans in a cold frame in May and the seedlings potted up singly. Repot until they are finally in 8 inch pots. Grow them in cool conditions, giving them ample ventilation. Plants may also be used out of doors in the border. Canterbury bells *(C. medium)* are raised in a shady site from seed sown in May or June. The bed should have a very fine tilth, and seed drills should be shallow; or sow in boxes in finely sieved soil and put the boxes in a frame, transplant seedlings to a nursery bed 6 inches apart. Set out in autumn where the plants are to flower, having added lime to the soil. *C. isophylla* and its varieties are propagated by cuttings taken in early summer and rooted in a greenhouse propagating frame. The plant does best in a cold greenhouse or conservatory as it is nearly hardy and, indeed, may survive out of doors in sheltered gardens. It may be used for planting in hanging baskets intended for outdoor decoration in summer.

Catananche (kat-an-an-kee)

From the Greek *katananke,* a strong incentive, referring to its use in love potions *(Compositae)*. A small genus of annuals or perennials of which *C. caerulea* is the only species likely to be found in cultivation. This is commonly known as Cupid's dart. It is a hardy perennial, 2½ feet tall, somewhat similar to a cornflower in habit of growth with gray-green leaves and light blue flowers surrounded by papery, silver colored bracts. It is a good border plant and is also an excellent cut flower, fresh or dried for winter decoration. It flowers from July to September. Improved forms are *major* and 'Wisley Variety'; var. *bicolor* has blue and white flowers; var. *alba,* a plant of very vigorous growth has large white flowers; 'Perry's White' is the best white cultivar, 'Snow White' is another excellent white kind.

Cultivation This perennial likes well drained soil and is not averse to lime. It should be given an open sunny position. Plant in October or March and provide adequate staking when plants are in full growth. It survives the winter best if a portion of the flower stems are removed at the end of August. Propagation is by division in March or by seed sown during April in a cold frame.

Celsia (sel-se-a)

Commemorating the famous theologian and botanist Olaf Celsius of Upsala *(Scrophulariaceae)*. A genus of perennials and biennials treated as half hardy annuals. They have tall spikes of yellow flowers in summer and look not unlike mulleins (verbascums).

Species cultivated: Greenhouse *C. arcturus,* 3 feet, perennial, flowers large, yellow with purple anthers, a good pot plant, Crete.

Hardy *C. cretica,* the Cretan mullein, 4 feet, biennial, fragrant golden-yellow flowers marked with brown, July and August, Mediterranean area.

Cultivation Seed of *C. arcturus* is sown in March, seedlings are potted singly and flowered in 8 inch pots. Seed of *C. cretica* is sown in the frame or in the cool greenhouse in March, the seedlings are pricked off and planted out at the end of May. Plants require staking. *C. cretica* may also be treated as a greenhouse biennial. Seed is sown in August to flower the following summer. Ample ventilation should be given.

Centaurea (sen-taw-re-a)

From the classical myths of Greece; the plant is said to have healed a wound in the foot of Chiron, one of the Centaurs *(Compositae)*. A genus of annual and perennial

Campanula latifolia alba is a white, summer flowering perennial that tolerates shade and is a tall, effective border plant.

plants with flowers not unlike those of a thistle in structure. The annuals (cornflowers and sweet sultana) are good for cutting; some species of perennials are used as foliage plants for the silvery-white leaves.

Perennial species cultivated *C. argentea,* semi erect, fernlike silvery leaves, pale yellow flowers, half hardy. *C. dealbata,* 3 feet, lobed leaves, silvery white beneath, pinkish-purple flowers, summer; var. *steenbergii,* flowers rosy-crimson. *C. glastifolia,* 5 feet, upright branching stems, pale yellow flowers, June and July. *C. gymnocarpa,* 1½ feet, subshrub, much lobed white leaves, half-hardy. *C. jacea,* 3—3½ feet, narrow leaves, rosy-purple flowers, summer. *C. macrocephala,* 2—3 feet, large yellow flowers, June to August, a good border plant. *C. maculosa,* 2½ feet, mauve flowers, summer. *C. montana,* 2 feet, deep blue flowers, April to June, easy to grow, one of the most popular; vars. *alba,* white; *rosea,* pink; *rubra,* rosy-red. *C. pulcherrima,* 2½ feet, narrow leaves, gray beneath, flowers bright rose pink, May to July. *C. ruthenica,* 4 feet, finely cut leaves, graceful plant, yellow flowers on long stems, summer. *C. rutifolia,* 3 feet, silver

foliage, yellow flowers, summer. *C. simplicicaulis*, 1 foot.
Cultivation Plant in fairly light soil including limestone soils. Propagation is by division in spring or by seed in midsummer.

Centranthus (ken-tran-thus)

From the Greek *kentron*, a spur, *anthos*, a flower, alluding to the shape of the flower *(Valerianaceae)*. A small genus of annuals and perennials, natives of Europe and the Mediterranean area. The hardy herbaceous perennial, *C. ruber,* the red valerian occasionally escapes cultivation, but is not a serious weed. The name is sometimes spelled Kentranthus.
Species cultivated *C. macrosiphon,* 2 feet, annual, flowers tubular, rose-pink, summer. *C. ruber,* red valerian, 2½ feet, reddish-pink flowers, June and July; vars. *alba,* white; *atro-coccineus,* deep red. All are handsome plants.

Chrysanthemum (kris-an-the-mum)

From the Greek *chrysos*, gold, *anthemon*, flower *(Compositae)*. A genus of over 100 species of annuals, herbaceous perennials and subshrubs, distributed over Africa, America, Asia and Europe. The well-known greenhouse and early flowering (outdoor) chrysanthemums are descended from *C. indicum,* found in China and Ja-

1 *Celsia arcturus is a half hardy shrubby perennial for the greenhouse.*
2 *Centaurea macrocephala is a hardy summer flowering plant native to the Caucasus.*
3 *Chrysanthemum rubellum is a hardy perennial variety. It has many good forms, including 'Clara Curtis', deep pink; 'Duchess of Edinburgh', fiery red; 'Mary Stoker', soft yellow and 'Paul Boissier', orange bronze.*

pan, and *C. morifolium* (syn. *C. sinense*), from China, two closely related, variable plants.
Hardy perennials *C. alpinum* 3—6 inches, white flowers, summer, Pyrenees, Carpathians, scree in rock garden. *C. argenteum* (syns. *Matricaria argentea, Pyrethrum argenteum, Tanacetum argenteum*), 6 inches, subshrubby, gray-white stems and leaves, solitary white flowers, summer. *C. cinerariifolium,* 1—2 feet, white flowers, July and August. This is the species which produces pyrethrum insecticide and is widely cultivated for this purpose in Japan and Kenya. *C. coccineum* (syn. *Pyrethrum roseum*), 2—3 feet, the pyrethrum of gardens, variable in color; the origin of the garden pyrethrum (see Pyrethrum). *C. haradjanii,* 6 inches, silvery leaves, rock garden foliage plant. *C. leucanthemum,* oxeye daisy, 2—3 feet,

*1 Convolvulus mauritanicus is a prostrate twining plant useful for hanging baskets.
2 Coreopsis verticillata is a hardy Tickseed reaching 2 feet in height.*

white flowers, summer, Europe and North America, a good cut flower. *C. maximum*, Shasta daisy, 1½—3 feet, white flowers, summer, Pyrenees; cvs. 'Beaute Nivelloise', fringed petals; 'Esther Read' double, the most popular; 'Horace Read', creamy white double; 'Ian Murray', anemone centered; 'Jennifer Read', later flowering; 'Mount Everest', large flowered; 'Thomas Killin', large anemone centered; 'Wirral Pride', double, lemon centered when first open; 'Wirral Supreme', large, double. Many others are to be found in catalogues and new varieties appear from time to time. *C. nipponicum*, 12—15 inches, white flowers, summer, Japan. *C. parthenium*, feverfew, 2 feet, pungent stems and leaves, white flowers, summer, best in its double form; var. *aureum*, golden feather, dwarf, yellow leaves, used in bedding. Flowerheads should be removed when they are finished flowering. *C. praeteritum*, 9 inches, subshrubby, gray, finely divided aromatic foliage; foliage plant. *C. ptarmicaefolium*, 1 foot, silvery-white, much divided foliage, white flowers, summer. Canary Islands. *C. rubellum*, 2—3 feet, single flowers, in shades of lilac and pink. September and October, of unknown origin; var. 'Clara Curtis', clear pink. *C. sibiricum* (syns. *C. coreanum* and *Leucanthemum sibiricum*), Korean chrysanthemum, 2—3 feet, variously colored flowers, single and double, September and October, Korea. *C. uliginosum*, giant daisy, moon daisy, 5 feet, single white flowers, autumn, good for cutting, eastern Europe.
Cultivation The taller hardy perennials are useful border plants which will grow in any ordinary soil and sunny position. They may be planted in spring or autumn and clumps should be lifted, divided and replanted every third year. The dwarf kinds are suitable for sunny rock gardens. All are propagated either by division in March or by seeds sown in the greenhouse at the same time.

Convolvulus (kon-volvu-lus)
From the Latin *convolvo*, to entwine, as some of the species do *(Convolvulaceae)*. A valuable race of plants both annual and perennial, herbaceous or subshrubby. Flowers are bell shaped throughout and highly attractive.
Hardy perennial species cultivated *C. althaeoides*, 1—2 feet, pink flowers, summer. *C. cantabrica*, 1 foot, pink flowers, mid to late summer. *C. cneorum*, 1—2 feet, silvery leaves, pinkish-white flowers, summer, subshrubby, a little tender. *C. incanus*, 6 inches, trailing, silvery leaves, bluish-white flowers, summer. *C. mauritanicus*, trailing, with blue flowers, summer, hardy in warm places, otherwise a fine plant for a greenhouse hanging basket. *C. tenuissimus*, 6 inches, silvery-gray leaves, bright pink flowers, late summer.
Cultivation These convolvulus can be grown in beds and borders and appreciate good soil and sun. Trailing species may be provided with support, if preferred. A sunny, sheltered rock garden is especially suitable for *C. cneorum*, *C. mauritanicus*

and other dwarf and trailing species. Propagation of hardier kinds is by seed sown out of doors in spring. Take cuttings of *C. cneorum* and *C. mauritanicus* in July and August. Plant in sandy soil in a frame. Bottom heat is an advantage.

Coreopsis (kor-e-op-sis)
From the Greek *koris*, a bug or tick, *opsis*, like, a reference to the appearance of the seeds *(Compositae)*. Tickseed. The annual species are often catalogued under *Calliopsis*. Hardy perennials and annuals with showy flowers, excellent for borders.
Perennial species cultivated *C. grandiflora*, 2—3 feet, yellow flowers, summer; var. *flore pleno*, double. Cultivars include 'Baden Gold', large golden yellow flowers; 'Mayfield Giant', orange-yellow; 'Sunburst', double yellow; 'Perry's Variety' semi double, clear yellow; 'Baby Sun', 1½ feet, golden-yellow. *C. lanceolata*, 2—3 feet, yellow flowers, summer; var. *grandiflora*, large flowered form. *C. major*, 2—3 feet, yellow flowers, mid to late summer. *C. palmata*, 1½—3 feet, orange-yellow flow-

Dahlias are among the most colorful flowers of late summer and early autumn, and they provide a wealth of material for cutting until the start of the cold frosty winter nights.

1 'Worton Jane' is a small flowered decorative Dahlia.

2 The blooms of Dahlia 'Amethyst Piper', a small-flowered decorative, may be as wide as 6 inches in diameter.

3 'Schweiz' is a medium decorative Dahlia.

4 'Harmari Girl' is a giant decorative Dahlia.

5 'Ruwenzori' is a popular and unusual Dahlia of the collarette type.

6 Dahlia 'Grand Prix' is a giant decorative.

7 'Beauty of Baarn' is a medium semi-cactus type of Dahlia, growing to 3½ feet in height, which holds its blooms high above the foliage.

ers, mid to late summer. *C. pubescens* (syn. *C. auriculata superba*), 2 feet, yellow and crimson flowers, summer. *C. rosea*. 9 inches—2 feet, pink flowers, summer. *C. verticillata*, 1½ feet, yellow flowers, summer; var. *grandiflora*, 2 feet, larger flowers.

Cultivation Coreopsis do well in ordinary well drained garden soil and in sunny positions. Plant perennials during autumn and spring. Propagate single perennial species from cuttings in April, or seed sown a month later; double forms by cuttings in April. Split large clumps in autumn. The annuals are raised from seed sown out of doors during spring and early summer, where they are intended to flower, thinning the seedlings to 9 inches. Alternatively, seed may be sown under glass at a temperature of 65°F in March.

Corydalis (kor-e-day-lis)

From the Greek *korydalis*, a crested lark, a reference to the shape of the flowers (*Fumariaceae*). Hardy annuals and perennials, widely distributed throughout the temperate regions of the northern hemisphere.

Perennial species cultivated *C. allenii*, 3—4 inches, pink and white flowers, spring. *C. cashmeriana*, 6 inches, blue flowers, spring. *C. cheilanthifolia*, 10 inches, yellow flowers, summer. *C. halleri* (syn. *C. solida*), 6 inches, purple flowers,

spring, tuberous rooted, native plant. *C. lutea*, 1 foot, yellow flowers, spring to autumn, native plant. *C. nobilis*, 1 foot, yellow flowers, early summer. *C. thalictrifolia*, 1 foot, yellow flowers, summer. *C. wilsonii*, 9 inches, yellow flowers, early summer.

Cultivation These plants thrive in ordinary soil in well drained, sunny positions. Ledges, nooks and crannies in rock gardens and walls are very suitable, as well as borders. Plant perennials in March. Propagate perennials by seed in early spring, or by division after flowering; tuberous rooted species by offsets in March.

Dahlia (day-le-a or dah-le-a)

Commemorating Andreas Dahl, a Swedish botanist who was a pupil of Linnaeus (*Compositae*). Half hardy, tuberous rooted perennials from Mexico.

Species cultivated (Few of the following original species are available, although they may occasionally be seen in botanic gardens and the like). *D. coccinea;* 4 feet, scarlet, September, the parent of the single dahlia. *D. coronata*, 4 feet, fragrant scarlet flowers on long stems, autumn. *D. excelsa*, 15—20 feet, purplish-pink flowers, summer. *D. gracilis*, 5 feet, scarlet-orange flowers, September. *D. juarezii*, 3 feet, parent of the cactus dahlias, flowers scarlet, late August and September. *D. merckii*, 3 feet, lilac and yellow flowers, October (to-

gether with *D. variabilis* the parent of most modern double dahlias). *D. variabilis*, 4 feet, (syns. *D. pinnata*, *D. rosea*, *D. superflua*), variable flower colors, even a green form was suspected at the end of the nineteenth century. The parent of show, fancy and pompon dahlias.

Cultivation Nowadays dahlias are comparatively easy to grow. They tolerate all soils between the moderately acid and alkaline and for ordinary garden purposes need little or no specialized attention, yet will flower profusely. In their evolution they have produced multiple types and hundreds of thousands of varieties simply because they are a cross pollinated plant. This means that it is possible to produce unusual and original cultivars by raising plants from seeds, which is an additional asset. Furthermore, with correct culture, plants will flower continuously from July until the first autumn frosts, providing a colorful display over a range of several months.

Soil preparation This begins in winter or early spring by digging of the site, at the same time incorporating plenty of bulky organic materials such as peat, leaf mold, vegetable compost, or well rotted manure, but use poultry manure sparingly, since it encourages too much growth at the expense of flowers. Put any of these into the top foot of soil, because dahlias make a mass of fibrous roots in this region. The organic materials can be mixed into the planting holes if only a few tubers or plants are grown, or if dahlias follow spring bedding plants, but generally it is better to mix them in the soil overall.

Before planting, top-dress the ground with a fertilizer containing a higher amount of potash in comparison with the nitrogen and phosphate content such as a 5—10—15. Root crop fertilizers have this analysis, and potato fertilizers are very good for the purpose. This application will provide the extra plant nutrients needed during growth, the organic materials previously supplied mainly providing humus for improving the soil conditions and water retention.

Type of stock The choice of stock will depend on the purpose which the plants are to fulfil. Dormant tubers are best for a garden display, for they flower earlier than dahlia plants and produce more flowers over the season as a whole. If you want extremely early flowers, for instance blooming in June, you can plant tubers in pots, or even in the greenhouse, in February. If you have protection, you can plant tubers out of doors in April and they will start to flower during early July. Remove the protection when danger of frost is past. In both these instances the best flowers will have bloomed before the growing season has finished. For the best results over the whole season, plant dormant tubers during the first half of May out of doors. They will not usually need protection, because by the time the shoots emerge above ground level it is likely that the threat of any late spring

7

frosts will be past. Nevertheless keep protective materials handy in case of occasional night frost at this time. Flowering will start in late July and early August depending on type.

There are two types of tuber, one being the ground root, a large bulky root resulting from growing a dahlia out of doors without restricting the roots. If replanted from year to year, the number of tubers tends to increase to excess, too many poor quality flowers result, and vigor and tuber formation decrease. Division every second year into several portions is advisable; each portion containing several growth buds, or eyes, and having at least one complete healthy tuber to start them into growth. (At this point, it may be noted that, unlike the potato, dahlia eyes are not on each individual tuber, but are congregated at the base of the old stems). An easy way to judge how many portions a root can be divided into is to put it in the greenhouse for two or three weeks. Spray overhead with water every second day until the shoots are about ½ inch long. Do not bury the tuber in any material as this will encourage unwanted root growth. With a knife cut the root into portions according to where the emerging shoots are grouped, or pry it apart.

The other type of dahlia tuber, the pot-grown or pot tuber, may be sold in general garden shops and stores in the spring. It is produced from cuttings made in early spring and grown in pots all through the season so that the roots are restricted and the tuber forms into a neat rounded mass. Although pot tubers are easy to store and transport, forming very good stock for the garden, they are not as good as ground roots for producing cuttings, generally having insufficient bulk to be divided. Pot tubers become ground roots after a season of growth out of doors and their planting times are the same as for ground roots. Before actual planting, chip away some of the wax coating if present to allow moisture to swell the tuber. All tubers may be planted until mid-June.

The dahlia plant itself, which provides a type of stock commonly sold by dahlia nurseries, is formed by rooting dahlia cuttings. Plants grown from cuttings flower later than those grown from tubers, though if you need early flowers before mid August, it is a good idea to specify on the order sheet 'April Delivery'. If you have a greenhouse or frame, you can then pot the plants into 5 inch pots and they will grow into fine bushy specimens by planting time. This is standard technique for large and giant flowered varieties.

You should not plant unprotected dahlia plants out of doors until danger of frost is past. In sheltered situations, free from late spring frosts, you can plant in late April or early May.

Planting This should be done by making a hole in the ground with a small spade. Stakes should be inserted at this time to avoid damaging the tubers if they are put

It is not difficult to keep Dahlias from one year to the next if simple precautions are observed. The Dahlia is a native of the warm Mexican climate: therefore, in cooler areas the tubers must be lifted in the autumn, dried and stored in a dry, frost free place.
1 Dahlia foliage is very sensitive to frost and will be blackened by the first frost.
2 Immediately after this occurs, cut down the plants to within about 9 inches of ground level.
3 Remove the tops and lift the plants with a fork, taking care not to spear the tubers in the process.
4 Shake off the soil and stand the tubers upside down in a dry, airy place to drain away the surplus sap.
5 Once the tubers are thoroughly dry, they can be stored in any dry frost free place.
6 Storing them in a bit of dry peat is not necessary, but it will help to exclude frost and absorb excess moisture.
7 Tubers should be stored where the temperature is 35−40°F.
8 Dahlias are usually propagated from cuttings made from shoots that grow from the old stems. These grow from the tubers, which are placed close together on a greenhouse bench and covered lightly with soil or peat to retain moisture.
9 Maintain a temperature of 60°F and take cuttings when the shoots are 2 to 3 inches long.
10 With a sharp knife, remove lower leaves.
11 Make a basal cut below a joint.
12 Insert the cuttings firmly with a dibble around the edge of a 3½ inch pot of sandy soil.
13 Each cutting should be clearly labelled with the name of the cultivar and watered. Then place the pots in the propagating house. Hormone rooting powders usually increase the number of cuttings that root while reducing the time. The inclusion of a fungicide helps reduce loss.

1 Pot grown Dahlias, raised from cuttings the previous spring, are sometimes sold for planting out. Grown in the open throughout the season, the tubers may develop into a neat rounded mass.
2 They should be cut down after the first frost, 3 dug up and dried off, and 4 stored in the normal way for re-planting.

water very frequently can be largely avoided even in the hottest weather if a thick mulch of straw is provided at the roots in mid July. This keeps down weeds as well as encouraging better root growth.

Tubers will need at least one strong stake, but dahlia plants grow better if they are supported by a triangle of three canes or stakes. Such plants have to carry all the weight of stems, leaves and flowers on one main stem, so are very prone to wind damage. Tubers on the other hand, push out rigid shoots from below soil level and are much less likely to be broken by the wind in the early stages of growth. These shoots should be tied to the stake every 18 inches, whereas the dahlia plant needs tying every 6 inches for additional protection. A good average length for dahlia supports is 5 feet; these are driven into the ground to a depth of 1 foot. Avoid having the stakes higher than the blooms because the wind will knock the flowers against them.

Ground tubers can be left to produce flowers on the tips of their main stems. Allow about eight main stems per division to emerge, and cut off any others below soil level carefully with a knife. Large and giant flowered varieties should be allowed to produce about five stems only.

Pot tubers, unless they produce sufficient main shoots from below soil level, will have to be treated like green plants. The leading growth tip of the plant is pinched out, or 'stopped', about a month after planting, usually when about six pairs of leaves have developed. This encourages sideshoots to be produced so plenty of flowers come into bloom as a start; otherwise, if not stopped in advance, dahlia plants produce one central flower only at first. Take notice which are the strongest emerging sideshoots after pinching, and when they are 3 inches long, remove the excess by snapping them out from their joins with the main stem. Retain five shoots only, however, with large and giant flowered varieties. The technique with the pot tuber is to select initially the strongest main shoot, similar to that of the dahlia plant as the central growing stem, removing the others. This main shoot will be pinched and the sideshoots selected in exactly the same way. A ground tuber is not usually pinched, the flowers being borne on the terminal, or crown buds of each stem. It can, however, be treated like a pot tuber or green plant as far as shoot growth is concerned, but by pinching and selecting one main stem, the flowers,

in later. The hole should be wide enough to prevent cramping and deep enough to allow the upper surfaces of the tubers to be about 2 inches below ground level. Replace the earth on top, shaking the tuber to settle it round the root as you proceed, firming it by gentle treading. This applies to both ground and pot tubers. Planting distances are 2 feet apart for pompons, 2½ feet for ball dahlias and all others, except the large and giant decoratives, such as cactus and semi-cactus, which should be 3 feet apart.

Keep the soil watered periodically to freshen the tubers and to start the shoots into growth. Shoots should emerge above the soil within five weeks; if not, dig up the tuber and inspect it for decay and slug damage. Slug pellets applied above soil level round the root when planting both tubers and plants are an advisable precaution. Dahlia plants are placed in a hole made with a trowel and their roots set so that the potting soil is just below ground level. Plastic or fiber pots, should be carefully removed from the plants before planting. (With peat pots especially, make sure

to keep the soil moist enough to encourage the roots to penetrate into the open ground, since failure to do this is a frequent cause of stunted, poorly growing plants). Again, it is important to support by a stake, previously driven in, thus avoiding damage to the roots. Moreover, arranging the stakes in a desired pattern can be a useful guide to design.

Summer Care The main requirement is copious watering, not a lot of feeding. Providing you have prepared the soil as suggested, all that will be needed during the growing period will be two topdressings of sulphate of potash, each at the rate of ¼ oz per square yard. One should be given at the first sign of the petal color opening from the bud, to improve stem strength and flower color; the other during early September to improve tuber formation. Monthly fertilization of liquid fertilizer is also very good and gives excellent results even if used for foliar feeding. The dahlia makes a number of leaves in August and even in very wet weather the soil may remain dry around the roots. The need to

Rooted cuttings are potted singly in 3 inch pots. When these are full of roots, plants may be transplanted to 5 inch pots or in the garden, weather permitting.
1 Place a crock over the drainage hole.
2 Cover with leaves or compost fiber.

3 Remove the plant gently.
4 Cover it gently but firmly with the soil mixture.
5 Leave room in the pot for watering.
6 Firm evenly and level off, keeping the plant covered until it is established.

through having to be produced on sideshoots, will be about three weeks later than on the tips of the main stems. Pompon varieties need no de-shooting or disbudding.

Disbudding should be done to all other types when the flower buds are about the size of a pea. Allow the main, centrally placed, largest bud to remain and flower on each shoot, removing the others, together with the fresh secondary shoots which will emerge from each leaf joint on the stem as the flowers mature. Leave just one, fairly low down, on each stem to produce the sucessive flower, again disbudding and de-shooting. This technique is adopted throughout the flowering period and is the only way to achieve a long flowering season combined with good quality flowers with long stems for cutting.

Left to their own devices, dahlias produce a mass of buds and flowers and soon become uncontrollable, their very tiny, poor blossoms often becoming single by the end of the season. If you need small flowered dahlias, grow special small flowered varieties.

Lifting and Storing Ideally this is done once frost has blackened the foliage. If, however, the autumn continues without frost, it does no harm to lift dahlias in late October and early November. Only in the mildest of places, in very sheltered situations or during unusually gentle winters can dahlias be left out of doors in the ground all winter. They can be put into a common storage place in the same way as potatoes, but the disadvantage here is that they may be killed if the weather becomes very severe. Furthermore, you cannot examine them for signs of rotting or put them in the greenhouse to take cuttings.

To lift dahlia roots, first cut off the stems just above soil level. Then lift by loosening in a circle with a broad tined fork, working well away from the stems. After lifting the roots clear of the soil, shake off as much adhering earth as possible. Then place the roots upside down in a well ventilated frame or shed for at least 10 to 14 days. During this period they will lose excess moisture and by the time the remaining soil becomes dust dry, they will be ready to be put into winter storage. There they should be covered with sacks or straw at night if frost threatens. Only in very wet autumns should artificial heat be used, never exceeding 70°F.

27

Before placing them in storage, retrim the stems as low as possible, without actually cutting into the tubers. Retie the labels on one of the tubers, because in storage the stems will become paper dry and will actually drop off. Most dahlia roots need no covering in storage, and in fact, a frequent cause of loss during the winter is covering them, putting them away and forgetting about them until the spring. Place them on racks in a frost proof shed, cellar, or in a location which can be kept frost free. Straw bales provide good frost protection.

Very tiny tubers, however, should be covered in boxes or pots with material such as peat or sand. During the winter, sprinkle the surface with water very occasionally if it gets dust dry, but avoid giving sufficient water to start the tubers into growth. A good temperature for storage is 40—50°F; it should never fall below 34°F nor exceed 50°F. If you must store them in a warm place, shrivelling is likely, so all tubers must then be covered by sand or soil in boxes, but keep the boxes separated and put only one layer of tubers in each box. Avoid any storage that is subject to drips or draughts, or is so airtight that it encourages fungus rot.

Every month inspect the tubers and if any parts are rotting, cut them out with a sharp knife. Dry the surfaces left with a rag and smear on captan or zineb to prevent further rot.

Pests and disease As a general precaution, always spray dahlias with insecticides every three weeks during the season of growth, including those growing in the greenhouse and frame.

Sometimes the soil becomes infected with verticillium wilt. When this occurs the stock must be destroyed and a fresh growing site found. Cauliflower-like growths, due to crown gall, also mean that affected stock must be destroyed, but it is slow to spread and healthy stock can still be grown in the same ground.

A common leaf disease, especially in humid summers, is dahlia leaf spot, causing light green ringed spots which later turn brown. In this event, treat the leaves with zineb.

Plants are sometimes attacked by virus diseases, in which light green patches or yellowing bands up the veins and perhaps dark green blisters on the leaves are symptoms. A more certain sign is dwarfing of the plant, which becomes very close-jointed and bushy, producing small flowers. Destroy stock affected in this way, for there is no cure at present.

1 Before planting Dahlias in the open, water thoroughly and take out a hole large enough to hold the rootball.
2 Knock the plant out carefully.
3 Position the roots just below the level of the soil.
4 Fill in the hole, firm evenly and leave a shallow depression for watering.

Common pests are aphids in summer, often migrating from beans, thrips and tarnished plant bug from time to time.

A difficult pest to control is the red spider mite which may attack some plants in dry seasons, causing yellow mottling. Frequent syringing under the leaves with water and spraying with malathion every ten days is the control routine to follow.

Earwigs are often a nuisance, eating holes in leaves and flowers. These can be controlled if you provide upturned pots, loosely filled with excelsior, straw, hay, etc., and placed on top of the canes or stakes; these should be emptied into boiling water.

Wasps sometimes make damaging attacks on dahlia flower stems and it is usually necessary to destroy the nest completely.

Propagation The preparation for growing from seed is a simple matter. Remove the petals as they fade and take the seed pods indoors before the frost, later extracting the seed and placing it in envelopes. The seed is sown in boxes in mid March, and the seedlings are potted in May and planted in June. The best breeding, however, is done by crossing selected varieties by hand, and covering the blooms with old nylon stockings to prevent chance pollination by bees and other insects. It should be remembered that dahlias do not come true to type or variety from seed, though dwarf bedding types, such as 'Coltness Gem' or 'Unwins Hybrids' are commonly grown in this way as they come reasonably true.

Years ago dahlia shoots were grafted to tubers to produce plants, but only research into virus control now employs this technique. Nowadays dahlias are commonly propagated from cuttings. Tubers are packed close together in boxes of soil in February, put on the greenhouse bench with bottom heat of about 60°F and watered. When the shoots, produced after some three weeks, are about 2½ inches long, they are cut off close to the tuber just below a leaf joint, and after removing the lower leaves, they are inserted into holes around the edge of 3 inch pots. Make holes by inserting a pencil sized dibble 1½ inches deep. The rooting medium is commonly sand or a mixture of equal parts of peat and sand. Five cuttings are placed in each pot. The pots are then placed over bottom heat from soil warming wires, pipes, or electrical heating cables. The temperature should be about 60°F around the pots. Cover the pots by suspending plastic sheeting above them in the daytime, plus paper if the sun shines, and spray them gently with water morning and night, removing the covers overnight. Do not make the mistake of overwatering the pots during the rooting period, or rotting may take place. Add water to the pot only when the sand surface dries out and then dip it in a bucket of water with a finger over the drainage hole until bubbles cease to rise. Otherwise, rely on overhead spraying on the cuttings themselves.

1

2

3

4

1 To encourage a bushy plant, take out the growing point when there are six pairs of leaves.
2 Three or four 'breaks' or side shoots will soon appear.
3 Old tubers may produce too many shoots, some of which may be removed.
4 Mulching with peat or compost retains moisture and controls weeds.

After two or three weeks, when new tip growth is evident, the cuttings will have rooted and can be potted individually in ordinary potting soil. For the first ten days keep them in a warm part of the greenhouse, but for the rest of the time until planting they grow much better if kept cool. Certainly they should be ready to be put into a cold frame three weeks after potting.

The division of tubers described earlier is the other method of propagation.

Types of dahlias There are now ten main groups, some being subdivided into sizes according to flower diameter. These in-

clude single flowered, anemone flowered, collerette, peony flowered and miscellaneous (containing such types as orchid flowered). As far as the gardener is concerned the most popular groups are the decorative dahlia, with flat broad petals; the cactus dahlia with petals that roll backwards to form a quill; semi cactus dahlias, which have only part of their petal length rolled; pompon dahlias, like drumsticks, their flowers having blunt, tubular petals, under 2 inches in diameter; and the new group of ball dahlias which comprise all the previously known groups of medium and large pompons and the similar, but

1 Dahlias require support from an early age, and a stout stake should be put in at planting time to avoid root injury.
2 Canes connected by string can be used to enclose the plant as it grows.
3 Large plants can be tied up in a circle of stakes.
4 Cut dahlias early in the morning.

large, double show varieties, plus any globular shaped varieties which were previously small or miniature decoratives.

Size groups are: pompons one size only; ball dahlias are divided into miniature balls, 2—3½ inches, and balls over 3½ inches, decorative, cactus and semi cactus dahlias are each divided into five groups; miniature, under 4 inches, small, 4—6 inches, medium 6—8 inches, large-flowered 8—10 inches, giant flowered over 10 inches. Bedding dahlias are put where their flower shape designates them.

Exhibiting Cultural technique varies little from that described. Cuttings are mostly used for propagation purposes; they flower during September when most dahlia shows are held. Tubers of the large flowered and giant varieties are started into growth in the greenhouse in mid January, cuttings being taken for rooting during early March; plants, when put in the frame, later on, should be put into 5 inch pots by early May. All other varieties are started in mid February, the best plants being obtained from cuttings rooted during the end of March and the first three weeks in April. Those taken before this period will usually flower much too early for the shows. For show work, it is much better to grow at

least six plants of each good variety, thereby restricting the number of varieties to the capacity of the outdoor space available in which to grow them. When garden plants are grown for display, distances should be 2 feet apart for pompons, 2½ feet apart for ball dahlias and all others, except the large and giant decoratives, cactus and semi cactus which should be placed 3 feet apart. Many exhibitors mulch the giant varieties, in July, with a straw mulch. During flowering it is common practice to protect the flowers of the large and giant varieties either with cones of builder's brown paper, or even by erecting metal uprights to support a roof made of corrugated vinyl clear plastic sheeting, giving the effect of an open sided greenhouse.

Always cut the flowers the evening before and keep them in a cool, dark place, in water, overnight. Large and giant blooms must have a 2 foot cane tied along the stem when it is cut to prevent the bloom toppling over in transit. It is always advisable to carry flowers to a show in water.

The best way to pick up showing techniques is to join a dahlia society if there is one in your locality, or if not, to contact the American Dahlia Society.

Delphinium (del-fin-e-um)

From the Greek *delphin,* a dolphin, the flower buds having some resemblance to that sea creature *(Ranunculaceae).* Larkspur. The genus consists of annual, biennial and herbaceous perennial plants, mostly hardy and showy plants for border cultivation, with some dwarf species suitable for the rock garden.

Perennial *D. brunonianum,* 1—1½ feet, light purple, June and July, western China. *D. cardinale,* 2—3 feet, bright red, July and August, California, somewhat tender. *D. denudatum,* 2½ feet, yellow and blue, summer, Himalaya. *D. elatum,* 2—3 feet, blue, June, Alps to Pyrenees eastwards, the plant from which most garden delphiniums have been derived. *D. formosum,* 3 feet, purple-blue, August, Caucasus, Asia Minor. *D. grandiflorum* (syn. *D. chinense*), 1—3 feet, violet-blue or white, long spurred, summer, Siberia. *D. nudicaule,* 1—1½ feet, red and yellow, April to June, California. *D. speciosum* (syn. *D. caucasicum*), 6 inches—2 feet, blue and purple, summer, Himalaya. *D. tatsienense,* 1½ feet, violet-blue, July, Szechwan. *D. vestitum,* 2 feet, pale and deep blue, summer, northern India. *D. zalil* (syn. *D. sulphureum*), 1—2½ feet, lemon-yellow, summer, Persia, requires a well drained soil.

Cultivation Sow annual varieties where they are to flower in a sunny, open border in April, or in boxes of light soil under glass in March at a temperature of 55°F. Prick off seedlings when large enough to handle and transplant in the open after danger of frost is past. Perennials should be planted in the spring or autumn in beds of rich,

1 Dahlia 'Lady Tweedsmuir' is a small flowered decorative.

2 Dahlia 'Coltness Gem' is a brightly colored flower of the collarette type.

1

2

3

4

deeply cultivated soil; dwarf varieties are suitable for rock gardens. Feed with liquid fertilizer in the early summer. Lift and replant every third year. Propagation of perennial varieties is by means of cuttings of young shoots in early spring, inserted in sandy soil in pots in a shaded propagating frame, or by seeds sown in the open ground in late spring or under glass in spring.

Cultivation of modern hybrid delphiniums Fast-growing plants, delphiniums require a deeply dug, rich soil with adequate drainage. A medium loam is preferable to a light sandy soil. Where the soil is light dig in deeply plenty of compost or old manure before planting and during the summer a mulch of garden compost is excellent. Nitrogenous fertilizers should

be used with care as they may only result in producing weak stems. If the stems are cut back immediately after flowering a second crop of spikes may be produced, but these should be encouraged only with strong growing varieties. Adequate moisture will be required to produce this second crop during what may be hot, summer weather. Delphiniums grow best in areas with cool summers. Slugs can be a menace with the tender young delphinium shoots, especially in the early spring, so precautions should be taken with slug pellets or other repellents. Varieties that grow to about 4—5 feet in height are more suitable for small gardens than those that tower to 7 feet or more, and they are less liable to damage by winds. Brushwood or

1 Delphiniums are easily propagated from cuttings taken from the emerging basal shoots.
2 Each shoot is removed with a sharp knife.
3 Up to six cuttings can be taken from one strong crown. Make a slanting basal cut below a leaf joint and remove the lower leaves.
4 Insert the cuttings firmly into sandy compost and place in a cold frame.

5 Porous vermiculite is a good rooting medium.
6 The cuttings should root quickly.
7 When ready, plant them out and protect them with a small cloche until set.
8 and 9 Caterpillars of the tortrix moth may attack the growing points.
10 Take precautions against damage.
11 Slugs and snails are also very partial to the new shoots of delphiniums.

twigs can be used to support the young growth but these should be put in position around the plants early so that the stems grow through them. This is often left until too late with the result that the tender stems get broken when the sticks are being pushed into the soil. Staking for exhibition must be carefully done, using one stout cane to each spike. When growing the large flowering varieties it is usual to restrict one year old plants to one spike and two year old plants to two or three spikes. Exhibition spikes should be straight, tapering and well filled with large circular florets but not overcrowded, and bearing few laterals. The foliage should be clean, healthy and undamaged. After spikes are cut they should be placed in deep contain-

ers filled with water and kept in a cool, but not draughty place. There they should remain for some hours or overnight. Each stem should be wrapped in a large sheet of tissue paper (30 × 40 inches) before being taken to the show. A further step to ensure that the spike does not wilt is to turn it upside down, immediately before final showing, fill the hollow stem with cold water and plug with cotton.

As they are easily raised from seed the delphinium has been of much interest to the plant breeder who has produced many stately varieties. The era of immense spikes has passed its zenith and the trend is to develop a range of hybrids not exceeding about 4½ feet in height. These are of much more general use in gardens which are ever becoming smaller but more numerous. From the glorious shades of blue the color range has been extended from white and cream through pink, carmine, mauve, lavender, purple and violet. Now, thanks to the work done by Dr. Legro, the celebrated Dutch hybridist, the range includes shades of cerise, orange, peach and tomato-red. Our garden hybrids have been mainly derived from *Delphinium elatum,* a natural tetraploid species, but Dr. Legro succeeded in overcoming the sterility barrier when he made a number of species crosses at diploid level, resulting in tetraploid plants and then successfully crossed to hybrid elatums. The rediscovery of the white African species, *D. leroyi,* which has a freesia like fragrance, also opens up pleasing possibilities. Many plant breeders are working on these problems and during the next few years we should see a truly remarkable range of hybrid delphiniums.

Recommended tall cultivars 'Alice Artindale', light blue, 6 feet; 'Ann Page', deep cornflower blue, 5½ feet; 'Bridesmaid', silvery-mauve, white eye, 7 feet; 'Charles F. Langdon', mid blue, black eye, 6½ feet;

1 Delphinium 'Daily Express'.
2 Delphinium 'Silver Moon' is one of the finest cultivars ever raised.

'Daily Express', bright sky blue, black eye, 6 feet; 'Janet Wort', pure white, 6½ feet; 'Jennifer Langdon', pale blue and mauve, 5½ feet; 'Mogul', rosy-purple, 6½ feet; 'Purple Ruffles', deep purple, overlaid royal blue, 5 feet; 'Royalist', deep blue, 6 feet; 'Silver Moon', silvery-mauve, white eye, 5½ feet; 'Swanlake', pure white, black eye, 5 feet.

Shorter-growing cultivars 'Blue Bees', pale blue, 4 feet; 'Blue Tit', indigo blue, black eye, 3½ feet; 'Blue Jade', pastel blue, dark brown eye, 4 feet; 'Cliveden Beauty', pale blue, 4 feet; 'Naples', bright blue, 4 feet; 'Peter Pan', deep blue, 3½ feet; 'Wendy', gentian-blue, 4—5 feet, the most

1 The dwarf Dianthus 'La Bourboulle' is a low growing plant only 3 inches high for the rock garden.
2 Dianthus 'Martinhoe' is happiest when planted in alkaline soil and exposed to full sun.

popular of the belladonna type.

The Pacific Hybrids raised in the U.S., growing 4—6 feet tall, include 'Astolat', lilac and pink; 'Black Knight' series, shades of violet; 'Blue Jay', mid blue; 'Cameliard' series, lavender shades; 'Elaine', rose-pink; 'Galahad' series, whites; 'Guinevere' series, shades of lavender-pink; 'King Arthur' series, shades of violet-purple; 'Lancelot' series, shades of lilac; 'Percival', white with a black eye; 'Round Table', including various colors as above; 'Summer Skies', good true blues.

Dianthus (di-an-thus)

From the Greek *dios,* a god or divine, *anthos,* a flower, divine flower, flower of Jupiter or Zeus *(Caryophyllaceae).* A large genus of hardy annual, biennial and perennial plants, which falls into three main groups: pinks, carnations and dianthus proper. The greatest number of species come from the Balkans and Asia Minor,

some from the Iberian Peninsula and North Africa, a few from China and Japan and two are natives of the British Isles. Many plants in the genus are very fragrant with a unique perfume, predominantly clove, strongest among the pinks and carnations. Many of the dwarf kinds are excellent rock garden plants; the taller kinds are suitable for sunny borders, banks or other places.

Species cultivated (All are perennial unless otherwise stated) *D. × allwoodii,* 6 inches—2½ feet, very variable in color, single and double, summer, hybrid. *D. alpinus,* 3 inches, rose-red, May and June, *D. arvernensis,* 4—6 inches, clear pink, May and June. *D. barbatus,* Sweet William, 6 inches — 1½ feet, perennial usually grown as a biennial, variable in color, summer. *D. × boydii,* 3—6 inches, rose-pink, May and July. *D. carthusianorum,* 1—1½ feet, rose-purple, June to August. *D. caryophyllus,* carnation, clove pink, picotee, 9 inches—3 feet, red, but very variable in cultivation, parent, with *D. chinensis,* of annual carnations and Chinese and Indian pinks. *D. chinensis* (syn. *D. sinensis*), Chinese or Indian pink, 9 inches, annual, variable in color, summer. *D. deltoides,* maiden pink, 6 inches, purple to crimson, spotted and striped, summer, native; vars. *albus,* white; *erectus,* rich red. *D. fragrans,* 1—1½ feet, white, summer, *D. gratianopolitanus* (syn. *D. caesius*), Cheddar pink, 1 foot, pink, May and June; vars. *albus,* white; *flore-pleno,* double or semi double. *D. haematocalyx,* 4—6 inches, bright pink, July. *D. knappii,* 1 foot, pure

Dicentra spectabilis, the Bleeding Heart, is a late spring flowering hardy perennial for the sun or shade. Its pendant flowers resemble lanterns hung along a cord.

yellow, July and August. *D. microlepis,* 2—3 inches, pink, flowers small, spring, scree plant. *D. monspessulanus,* 6—12 inches, pink, summer. *D. musalae,* 2 inches, bright pink, spring. *D. myrtinervis,* 2—3 inches, pink, small, spring. *D neglectus,* 3 inches, rose-red, June, dislikes lime. *D. nitidus,* 6 inches—2 feet, rose-pink, July and August. *D. noeanus,* 6—8 inches, white, July and August. *D. petraeus* (syn. *D. kitaibelii*), 8—12 inches, pink, June; var. *albus,* 6 inches, double white. *D. pindicola,* 2 inches, deep pink, summer. *D. plumarius,* pink, Scotch pink, 1 foot, variable in color, May to July. Parent of the garden pinks. *D. squarrosus,* 1 foot, white, summer. *D. sternbergii,* 6 inches, rose-red, June, *D. strictus,* 6 inches, white, June and July. *D. subacaulis,* 3 inches, rose-pink, June to August.

Cultivars are numerous. Those of species described above include 'Ariel' ('Crossways'), 4—6 inches, cherry red, July and August; 'Baker's Variety', 6 inches, large, deep pink, June and July; *D. deltoides* 'Brilliant', 6 inches, crimson, summer, and 'Huntsman', 6 inches, bright red, June and July; 'Charles Musgrave', 9 inches, white with green eye, summer; 'Cherry Ripe', 6—9 inches, rose-red, summer; *D. gratianopolitanus* 'Prichard's Variety', 4—6 inches, rose pink; 'La Bour-

boulle', 3 inches, deep pink, summer, and 'Double Ruby', 9 inches, summer; 'F. C. Stern', 6 inches, rosy-red, June to September; 'Fusilier', 3 inches, shining crimson, summer; 'F. W. Millward', 9 inches, double pink, summer; 'Highland Queen', 1 foot, deep rose, summer; 'Holmsted', 6 inches, soft pink, summer; 'Inchmery', 1 foot soft pink, double, summer; 'Isolde', 9 inches, pink and white, double, summer; 'Len Hutton', 1 foot, claret-red, edge laced white, summer; 'Little Jock', 4 inches, rose-pink with darker eye, semi double, summer; 'Little Jock Hybrids', various colors; 'Margaret Curtis', 1 foot, white, crimson zone, summer; 'Mars', 4 inches, rich red, double; 'Spencer Bickham', 4 inches, deep pink, summer; 'Sweet Wivelsfield' *(D. × allwoodii × D. barbatus)*, 18 inches, half hardy annuals in many bright colors, summer; 'Windward Rose', 6 inches, light rose, summer.

Cultivation Good drainage and preferably a limy soil in a sunny position is needed for most dianthus, except perhaps *D. alpinus* which likes less sun and tolerates an acid soil fairly well, and *D. neglectus* which dislikes alkaline soil. All do well in sandy loam. When the alpine species are grown in pots in the alpine house a compost ensuring adequate drainage but at the same time sufficiently retentive of moisture is needed. Make it of 2 parts of coarse sand or crushed gravel, 2 parts of leaf mold, 1 part of loam and a scattering of bone meal. Cover the surface of the pots with stone chips for attractiveness, to present the plant as a perfect cushion and to guarantee surface drainage. Propagation is from seed for annual and biennial kinds and those species that produce seed, or by cuttings taken immediately after flowering and inserted in clean sand around the edges of a pot and protected until rooting has taken place.

Dicentra (di-sen-tra)

From the Greek *di,* two, *kentron,* a spur, referring to the two spurs on the petals *(Fumariaceae).* Hardy herbaceous perennials formerly known as *Dielytra.* Fibrous and tuberous rooted, they generally transplant with difficulty because the roots are brittle. The flowers are pendant from arching stems, like lanterns hung along a cord.

Species cultivated *D. cucullaria,* Dutchman's breeches, 6 inches, very divided pale green foliage, flowers pearl white, tipped yellow, May and June. *D. eximia,* 1—1½ feet, reddish-purple flowers, May to September; var. *alba,* white flowers. *D. formosa,* 1—1½ feet, pink or light red, long flowering period; 'Bountiful' is a larger-flowered cultivar, with deep pink flowers. *D. oregana,* 6 inches, flowers creamy-pink, tipped purple, May and June. *D. peregrina* (syn. *D. pusilla*), 3 inches, rose-pink flowers in June and July, a good plant for a scree in the rock garden. *D. spectabilis,* bleeding heart, 1½—2 feet, flowers rose-red, May and June; var. *alba,* white, a garden hybrid *(D. eximia × D. formosa),* 9—12 inches has deep red flowers.

Cultivation Dicentras will grow in light shade or full sun provided the soil does not dry out. A rich loam is best with shelter from cold winds. Some protection may be needed in winter. Propagation is by root cuttings in March or April at a temperature of about 55°F. Division of plants is possible in spring, but difficult because the roots are very brittle. *D. spectabilis* is sometimes grown in pots and forced in a compost of equal parts of loam, peat and sand. The plants are kept frost free all winter and taken into a temperature of 55—65°F during February and started into growth. Water, and feed moderately with a liquid fertilizer when the buds begin to show. Forced plants should be planted out in the open after they have flowered and danger of frost has passed.

Dichorisandra (di-kor-iss-and-ra)

From the Greek *dis,* twice, *chorizo,* to part, *aner,* anther, referring to the 2 valved anthers *(Commelinaceae).* A genus of herbaceous perennial plants from tropical America, grown mainly for their ornamental foliage, though some also have showy flowers. They need greenhouse culture in northern areas.

Species cultivated *D. mosaica,* 2 feet, leaves green with white veins and other marks, reddish-purple on the undersides, flowers bright blue, autumn, Peru. *D. pubescens,* 2 feet, flowers blue; var. *taeniensis,* leaves striped with white, flowers blue and white, Brazil. *D. thyrsiflora,* 4 feet or more, leaves dark green, flowers dark blue in a 6 inch long spike, summer to autumn, Brazil. *D. vittata,* 6—12 inches, leaves purplish-green with white stripes, Brazil.

Cultivation These plants are potted in March in a soil mixture consisting of loam, leaf mold and peat in equal parts, plus a little sand. The pots should be in the warmest part of the greenhouse, where a winter temperature of 55—65°F can be maintained, rising in summer to 75—85°F, when shading from sunlight should be provided. Water freely from spring to autumn, moderately only in winter and avoid draughts at all times. Propagation is by seeds sown in the spring, by division of the plants in March or by cuttings taken at almost any time, rooted in a propagating case with bottom heat.

Dipsacus (dip-sa-kus)

From the Greek *dipsao,* to thirst, a reference to the water-holding cavity formed by the leaves united around the stem *(Dipsaceae).* Teasel. Biennial or perennial herbs, stiff, erect, rough plants with spiny or prickly stems and fruits; a European plant now naturalized in central and northeastern United States. The heads have long been used to tease wool and raise the pile on cloth. They are also useful in dried flower arrangements for winter decoration.

Species cultivated *D. fullonum,* fuller's teasel, 3—6 feet, flowers delicate mauve in conical heads from June to August, bien-

1 *Dichorisandra thyrsiflora is a summer flowering native of Brazil.*
2 *Dipsacus sylvestris, the Teasel, is an attractive everlasting perennial.*

nial. *D. sylvestris,* common teasel, 5—6 feet, flowers pale lilac, summer, a biennial plant.

Cultivation Alkaline well drained soils in open sunny situations are best, but tolerate many soil types. Propagation is from seed sown in the open in May or June. The seedlings are thinned and transplanted to their permanent positions in September to flower the following year. No staking is required, but the plants need plenty of room and should be set not less than 2 feet apart. The flower heads should be cut with long stems any time in the late autumn and stored, wrapped in paper or plastic to keep them dust free, in a dry place until required. They can be gilded or silvered for indoor or Christmas decoration. Left unpainted they dry to a pleasant autumnal brown.

Doronicum (dor-on-ik-um)

From the Arabic name *doronigi (Compositae).* Leopard's bane. Hardy herbaceous perennials, natives of Europe and Asia, early flowering, with long stemmed, daisy like yellow flowers. The sap from the root of *D. pardalianches* is said to be poisonous. Doronicums last well as cut flowers.

Echinacea (ek-in-ay-se-a)
From the Greek *echinos*, hedgehog, referring to the whorl of prickly, pointed bracts close beneath the flower head *(Compositae)*. A genus of two North American species of hardy herbaceous perennial plants.

Species cultivated *E. angustifolia* (syn. *Rudbeckia angustifolia*), 2—3 feet, purplish-red, summer. *E. purpurea* (syn. *Rudbeckia purpurea*), purple coneflower, 3—4 feet, purplish-red, August. The crimson cultivar 'The King', 6 feet tall, is outstanding, with flowers 5 inches across from August to October. 'Robert Bloom', is a newer cultivar, 3 feet tall, with large, carmine-purple flowers in July and August. Other named cultivars appear from time to time in nurserymen's lists.

Cultivation Plant in autumn or spring in a deep, rich, light loamy soil and in a sunny position. Propagation is by division in spring; by root cuttings in February, or by seed sown in boxes of light soil in March at a temperature of about 55°F, or sown out of doors in a sunny position in April.

1 *Doronicum plantagineum excelsum*, sometimes called 'Harpur Crewe's Variety', is a tall hardy perennial.
2 *Erigeron 'Foerster's Liebling' is a semi double form.*
3 *Echinacea purpurea, the Purple Coneflower, is a fine border plant.*

Species cultivated *D. austriacum,* 18 inches, golden-yellow, spring. *D. carpetanum,* 2 feet, yellow. May and June. *D. caucasicum,* 1 foot, yellow, April and May; var. *magnificum,* flowers larger. *D. clusii,* 1 foot, yellow, May and June. *D. cordatum,* 6—9 inches, deep yellow, April and May. *D. orientale,* 1 foot, yellow. April. *D. plantagineum,* 2—3 feet, yellow, spring; var. *excelsum* (syn. 'Harpur Crewe') larger, bright yellow flowers, April to June. Other good named types will be found in nurserymen's catalogues. The new German hybrid 'Fruhlingspracht', or 'Spring Splendor', 1 foot, is an interesting introduction with double yellow flowers during April and May.

Cultivation Plant in the autumn or spring in ordinary garden soil in sun or partial shade. Propagation is by division in October or March. Doronicums are adaptable plants which may be moved or divided without damage even when they are in bud, provided this is done in moist weather.

Echinops (ek-in-ops)

From the Greek *echinos,* a hedgehog, *opsis,* like, referring to the spiky appearance of the flower heads which resemble a rolled up hedgehog *(Compositae)*. Globe thistle. Hardy herbaceous perennial and biennial plants for the border.

Species cultivated (All perennial) *E. bannaticus,* 2—3 feet, violet-blue globular heads of flowers, summer, Hungary. *E. humilis,* 3—5 feet, large blue heads, September, Asia; var. *nivalis,* white. The cultivar 'Taplow Blue' has bright blue heads in summer. *E. ritro,* 3—4 feet, steel blue, summer, southern Europe. *E. sphaerocephalus,* 6 feet, flowers silvery-gray, summer, Europe and western Asia.

Cultivation Plant in autumn or spring in ordinary soil, in sun or partial shade. Echinops are trouble free plants for a large border or for a wild garden. The metallic luster of the flower heads keeps them decorative for a long time when dried. The species *E. ritro* is probably the best for this purpose. Propagation is by root cuttings or division in October or March, or by seed sown in the open in a sunny position in April.

Erigeron (er-ij-er-on)

From the Greek *eri,* early or *ear,* spring *geron,* old, possibly referring to the hoary leaves of some species *(Compositae)*. Fleabane. Hardy herbaceous, daisy flowered perennials some of which continue to flower intermittently throughout the summer.

Species cultivated *E. alpinus,* 9 inches, purple and yellow, August, northern Alps. *E. aurantiacus,* orange daisy, 12—18 inches, orange, summer, Turkestan. *E. aureus,* 4 inches, bright gold, spring onwards, North America. *E. compositus,* 3 inches, purple, summer, North America. *E. glaucus,* 6—12 inches, purple to pink, summer, North America. *E. coulteri,* 15 inches, white or pale mauve, summer, North America. *E. leiomerus,* 4 inches, small, lavender-blue, North America. *E. macranthus* (syn. *E. mesa-grande*), 2 feet, violet, yellow centers, summer, North Africa. *E. mucronatus,* 9 inches, white, deep and pale pink, summer and autumn, Mexico, a useful wall plant. *E. philadelphus,* 2 feet, lilac-pink, summer, North America. *E. speciosus,* 18 inches, violet-blue, summer, North America. *E. trifidus,* 2 inches, pale lavender, summer, North America. *E. uniflorus,* 4 inches, white or purplish, summer, North America.

Cultivars include: 'B. Ladhams', 1½ feet, bright rose; 'Bressingham Strain', *(E. aurantiacus),* 1—1½ feet, orange to yellow shades, May to July; 'Charity', 2 feet, pale pink; 'Darkest of All', 2 feet, deep violet; 'Dignity', 2 feet, mauve-blue; 'Felicity', 1½—2 feet, deep pink, large; 'Foerster's Liebling', 1½ feet, deep pink, semi double; 'Gartenmeister Walther', 2 feet, soft pink; 'Merstham Glory', 2 feet, deep lavender-blue, semi double; 'Prosperity', 2 feet, deep blue; 'Quakeress', 2 feet, pale blue overlaid silvery pink; 'Quakeress White', 2 feet, white; 'Unity', 2 feet, bright pink; 'Vanity', 3 feet, clear pink, late flowering; 'Wupperthal', 2 feet, pale blue.

Cultivation Plant in the autumn or early spring in a sunny position in ordinary soil in a rock garden, or towards the front of the border for the taller varieties. *E. mucronatus* is a good plant for paved areas or steps, where it can seed itself between the cracks. Cut down stems after flowering. Named varieties are propagated by division of the clumps in the autumn or spring, the species by seed sown in the open in light soil in a shady position from April to June.

Erodium (er-o-de-um)

From the Greek *erodios,* a heron; the style and ovaries resemble the head and beak of a heron *(Geraniaceae)*. Heron's bill. Hardy perennials, closely related to the hardy geraniums, or crane's bills. Dwarf species

1 Erodium corsicum forms a mat of summer flowers.
2 Eryngium maritimum, the Sea Holly, is an everlasting hardy perennial.

branches, June to August, Pyrenees. *E. bromeliifolium,* 3—4 feet, long, slender leaves, flowers pale green to white, July hardy in the south and west, Mexico. *E. dichotomum,* 1—2 feet, blue, July and August, southern Europe. *E. giganteum,* up to 4 feet, rounded blue heads, July and August, Caucasus. *E. heldreichii,* 1—2 feet, bluish, summer, Syria. *E. leavenworthii,* 3 feet, purple, summer, North America. *E. maritimum,* sea holly, 1—1½ feet, pale blue, summer to autumn, Europe, including Britain. *E.* × *oliverienum,* 3—4 feet, teasel like, metallic blue flowers, July to September, a hybrid. *E. pandanifolium,* 6—10 feet, narrow, spiny leaves up to 6 feet in length, purple-brown flowers, late summer, Uruguay, hardy in the south and west. *E. planum,* 2 feet, small, deep blue flowers, July and August, eastern Europe. *E. serra,* 6 feet, leaves up to 5 feet long, narrow, with spiny teeth, flowers white to pale green, autumn, Brazil. *E. spinalba,* 1—2 feet, small bluish-white flowers, summer, Europe. *E. tripartitum,* 2—2½ feet, steel blue, with long bracts, summer, possibly a hybrid, origin unknown. *E. variifolium,* 1½—2 feet, leaves white veined, flowers whitish-green, summer, Europe. Cultivars include 'Blue Dwarf', 2 feet; 'Violetta', 2½ feet, violet-blue, both flowering in late summer.

Cultivation Plant in the autumn or in the spring, preferably in light sandy soil, although these plants are not particular, so long as the drainage is good. They like a sunny site and dislike cold, wet soil in winter. The thong like roots require the soil to be deeply cultivated. Generally speaking, eryngiums from South America are half hardy or hardy in warmer areas only. They are, however, striking plants where they can be grown. Propagation is by seed sown in boxes and placed in a cold frame in April or May; by division of the plants in October or April, or by root cuttings.

are suitable for the rock garden and taller border plants.

Species cultivated *E. absinthoides,* 1 foot or more, violet, pink or white, summer, southeast Europe, Asia Minor; var. *amanum,* 6 inches, white, leaves hairy white. *E. chamaedryoides* (syn. *E. reichardii*), 2 inches, white, veined pink, June, Majorca; var. *roseum,* deep pink. *E. chrysanthum,* 6 inches, soft yellow flowers, summer, gray-green, ferny leaves, Greece. *E. corsicum,* mat forming, rosy-pink with deeper veins, summer, Corsica; vars. *album,* white, *rubrum,* clear red. *E.* × *kolbianum,* 3 inches, white to pink, summer, hybrid. *E. loderi,* 4—6 inches, white or pale pink, summer. *E. macradenum,* 6 inches, violet, blotched purple at base, summer, Pyrenees. *E. manescavii,* up to 2 feet, wine-red, summer, Pyrenees. *E. pelargoniflorum,* 1 foot, white, marked purple, summer, Anatolia. *E. supracanum,* 4 inches, white, veined pink, summer, Pyrenees.

Cultivation Plant the taller varieties in March or April in ordinary soil and in a sunny position. These plants dislike acid soils. They seldom need transplanting, although pot grown alpine species should be repotted in April every year, in a compost of equal parts of loam, leaf mold, and sharp sand. Propagation is by seed sown in March or April for the taller species at a temperature of 55°F and in July or August

Erysimum rupestre is a spring flowering rock garden perennial.

in a cold frame for the alpine species. Plants may be divided in April, and cuttings of dwarf species for the rock garden may be taken in May. The cuttings should then be rooted in a sandy soil, in a frame.

Eryngium (er-in-je-um)

From the ancient Greek name *eryngeon,* the meaning of which is obscure *(Umbelliferae).* A genus of over 200 species of hardy and nearly hardy perennial herbaceous plants, some with thistle like leaves. Some species are seaside plants in the wild. All are more or less spiny and in some species a feature is the glistening, metallic bluish sheen that covers the stem, the inflorescence, and the floral bracts. If the stems are cut and allowed to dry slowly they retain their color and sheen, thus providing useful winter decoration.

Species cultivated *E. agavifolium,* 5—6 feet, narrow spiny leaves up to 5 feet in length, flowers green, hardy in milder countries, Argentine. *E. alpinum,* 1—1½ feet, upper parts tinged blue, summer, Europe. *E. amethystinum,* up to 2½ feet, deep blue shiny flower heads and upper stems, July to September, Europe. *E. bourgatii,* 1½—2 feet, leaves marked gray-white, flowers light blue on spreading

Erysimum (er-is-im-um)

From the Greek *erus,* to draw up; some species are said to produce blisters *(Cruciferae).* Alpine wallflower. Hardy annual, biennial and perennial plants, closely related to *Cheiranthus.* Some are rather weedy, but others make good edging plants for a perennial border, or on gravelly banks and retaining walls.

Annual species cultivated *E. perofskianum,* 1 foot, reddish-orange, summer, Afghanistan.

Biennial *E. allionii* see *Cheiranthus allionii,* *E. arkansanum,* 1½—2 feet, golden-yellow, July to October, Arkansas and Texas. *E. asperum,* 1 foot, vivid orange, early summer, North America. *E. linifolium* (syn. *Cheiranthus linifolius*), 1—1½ feet, rosy-lilac, early summer, Spain.

Perennial *E. dubium* (syn. *E. ochroleucum*), 1 foot, pale yellow, April to July, Europe. *E. rupestre,* 1 foot, sulphur-yellow, spring, Asia Minor.

1

2

Cultivation The alpine wallflowers like ordinary soil in dryish, sunny beds or in the rock garden. Propagation of annuals is by seed sown in April where the plants are to flower; biennials by seed sown out of doors in June in a sunny place, transplanting the seedlings to their flowering positions in August; perennials by seed sown in a similar manner or by division in March or April, or by cuttings inserted in sandy soil in August in a cold propagating frame.

Euphorbia (u-for-be-a)

Named after Euphorbus, physician to King Juba of Mauritania *(Euphorbiaceae).* A genus of about a thousand species, widely distributed, mainly in temperate regions, showing immense diversity of form and requirements. They include annual, biennial and perennial herbaceous plants, shrubs and trees and succulent plants. The decorative parts are really bracts, often colorful, around the small and inconspicuous flowers. Some are warm greenhouse plants; others are hardy. The succulent species are mainly from Africa, most of them from South and West Africa. Many of those resemble cacti in appearance. All euphorbias exude a poisonous milky latex when the stems are cut, which can burn the skin and eyes and which, in some species, is poisonous if taken internally.

Greenhouse species cultivated (all non-succulent), *E. fulgens* (syn. *E. jacquinaeflora*), 2—3 feet, small leafy shrub, scarlet bracts carried on the upper side of young shoots, autumn and winter, Mexico. *E. pulcherrima* (syn. *Poinsettia pulcherrima*), poinsettia, 3—6 feet, brilliant scarlet, white or pink showy bracts in winter, Mexico. The modern Ecke hybrids are increasing in popularity. They include 'Barbara Ecke', fluorescent carmine bracts; 'Pink Ecke', coral pink and 'White Ecke', white. Some have variegated foliage. Even more popular now is the Mikkelsen strain, introduced in 1964. These, with shorter stems and with bracts in scarlet, pink or

1 Euphorbia epithymoides makes a colorful spring bedding plant.
2 Euphorbia obesa is distinguished by unusual plaid like markings.

white, are a good deal 'hardier' in that they will withstand lower temperatures and fluctuating temperatures, yet will retain their bracts and remain colorful for 5—6 weeks or longer.

Hardy *E. biglandulosa,* 2 feet, yellow, February and March, Greece. *E. cyparissias,* cypress spurge, plowman's mignonette, 1—2 feet, small narrow leaves, small greenish-yellow flowers and yellow, heart shaped bracts, May, Europe. *E. epithymoides* (syn. *E. polychroma*), cushion spurge, 1—1½ feet, rounded heads of golden-yellow bracts, early April to late May, Europe. *E. griffithii,* 1½—2 feet, reddish-orange flowers and bracts, April and early May; the cultivar 'Fireglow' has redder flower heads, Himalaya. *E. heterophylla,* Mexican fire plant, annual poinsettia, 2 feet, scarlet bracts, annual, North and South America. *E. lathyrus,* caper spurge, 3 feet, large green bracts, biennial, Europe. *E. marginata,* snow-on-the-mountain, 2 feet, leaves banded white, bracts white, annual, North America. *E. myrsinites,* trailing, good when sprouting between stones of a dry wall, fleshy stems, blue-gray foliage, bright yellow flower heads, late winter and spring, southern Europe. *E. pilosa,* 18 inches, usually grown in its form *major,* with yellow foliage, turning bronze in autumn, Europe, north Asia. *E. portlandica,* 9 inches, blue-green leaves, yellow bracts, British native. *E. robbiae,* 1½ feet, rosettes of dark green leaves, bracts yellow, good ground cover plant for shade. *E. sikkimensis,* 2—3 feet, young shoots bright red, bracts yellow-green, summer, India. *E. veneta* (syn. *E. wulfenii*), to 4 feet, nearly 3 feet across, very handsome almost subshrubby plant, gray-green foliage, yellow-green flower heads

with black 'eyes', spring to summer, Europe. Other species and varieties of hardy spurges may be found in nurserymen's catalogues.

Succulent There are very many species in cultivation: some of the following are some of the more popular ones, *E. alcicornis,* to 2 feet, leafless, spiny shrub, stem five angled, Madagascar. *E. bupleurifolia,* dwarf, thick stem like a tight fir cone, large deciduous leaves growing from the top, pale green flowers, Cape Province. *E. canariensis,* shrub with small yellow flowers, many erect stems, 4—6 ribbed, short spines on edges, Canary Isles. *E. caput-medusae,* dwarf, thick main stem, making a large head from which radiate many thin branches a foot or more long, small yellow flowers. There is a cristate or monstrous form with thin, flattened branches, Cape Province. *E. echinus,* shrub with erect stem and many branches, 5—8 angled, stems similar in shape to the cactus, *Cereus eburneus,* south Morocco. *E. obesa,* one of the most popular euphorbias, plants round when young, colored like plaid, becoming columnar, closely resembling the cactus, *Astrophytum asterias;* this plant does not make offsets so must be grown from seed, Cape Province. *E. splendens,* crown of thorns, 2—3 feet, succulent, spiny, few leaved shrub, pairs of round scarlet bracts, mainly in spring, Madagascar.

Cultivation: Greenhouse (non-succulent) species A good soil mixture is 4 parts of fibrous loam, 1 part of organic matter such as peat and a half part of sand. Young plants should be potted in 6 inch pots in summer and kept in a greenhouse or frame until September. Feed regularly with a liquid fertilizer and bring into a temperature of 60—65°F to bring the plants into flower in December. After flowering, keep growing by regular watering. In April cut back to two buds. Repot in May when the young shoots are about 1 inch long. Propagation is from cuttings of young shoots taken in July to mid September, and

inserted in sand at a temperature of 70°F.
Hardy species Any good garden soil suits
them. *E. veneta (E. wulfenii)* prefers a
slightly sheltered position, but the others
should be given sunny places. The dwarf
kinds are suitable for the rock garden, al-
through *E. cyparissias* tends to go wild,
spreading by underground rhizomes.
Propagation of perennial kinds is by division of the plants in spring or autumn but
E. veneta is best increased from seed or soft
cuttings taken in early spring and inserted
in a sandy soil out of doors or in a
greenhouse. The annuals and the biennial,
E. lathyrus, are easily raised from seed
sown out of doors in April where the plants
are to flower, thinning the seedlings later.
E. lathyrus seeds itself freely.
Succulent species Most of these plants
like a richer soil than some succulents but
it must be porous. The soil should be made
of a good potting mixture with a fifth part
added of sharp sand, grit or broken brick.
Repot in March every two years or when
the plants become pot bound; water well
from April to September, keep fairly dry
from October to March. Temperatures
should be 65°F, in the growing period,
45—50°F in winter. Plants should be given
a light sunny place in the greenhouse or on
a window sill. Propagation is by seed sown

*Gaillardia 'Goblin' with its crimson center
bordered with yellow is, like others of its
kind, a gay and colorful border plant for
late summer effect.*

in early spring. Cover the seed with soil,
keep moist at temperature of 70°F, shade
from sun but give light when seedlings appear. Large seeds should be washed well
before sowing. Plants may also be propagated by cuttings which should be dusted
with powdered charcoal to prevent bleeding, then dried and rooted in sharp sand
and peat in equal parts. Pot the cuttings
when they have rooted using a loam peat
mixture.

Gaillardia (gail-ar-de-a)
Named for M. Gaillard de Marentonneau,
a French patron of botany *(Compositae).*
Blanket flower. A small genus of annuals
and perennials, natives of America, with a
long flowering period, useful for cut flowers. Somewhat untidy in habit, the long
stalks fall about in wind and rain. Gaillar-
dias may need some twiggy stakes to help
to keep the flowers clean and in full view.
Annual species cultivated *G.
amblyodon,* 2—3 feet, maroon-red flowers,
autumn. *G. pulchella,* 2—3 feet, crimson

and yellow flowers, late summer and autumn, best treated as a half hardy annual;
vars. *brenziana,* double flowers in reds and
yellows; *picta,* larger flower heads. 'Indian
Chief' with coppery-scarlet flowers is a
named cultivar. In addition seedsmen usually offer mixed annual types under such
names as 'Choice Double Mixed', 'Special
Mixture', and 'Double Fireball'.
Perennial species cultivated All garden
varieties originate from *G. aristata* (syn. *G.
grandiflora*) and comprise a great range of
color from pale primrose yellow to crimson
and bold orange, all flowering from June to
October. Named cultivars include 'Bur-
gundy', 2 feet, rich wine red with a narrow
yellow frill along the outer edges of the
petals; 'Copper Beauty', 2 feet, smaller
flowers of orange-yellow suffused with
brown; 'Dazzler', 2 feet, yellow with
brown-red central zone; 'Firebird', 2 feet, a
vigorous variety with flame orange flowers; 'Goblin', 1 foot, dwarf, yellow with red
zone; 'Ipswich Beauty', 2½—3 feet, large
deep yellow flowers touched with reddish-
brown; 'Monarch Strain', 2½ feet, mixed
colors; 'Nana Nieski', 1—1½ feet, red and
yellow flowers on shorter stems; 'The
Prince', 2½ feet, very large flowers up to 4
inches across, deep yellow tinged reddish-
brown at the center; 'Tokaj', 2 feet, wine-

red and tangerine; 'Wirral Flame', 2½ feet, a strong growing variety, tangerine flowers tipped yellow; 'Yellow Queen', 2 feet, golden-yellow.

Cultivation A sunny border in a moderately light soil is ideal and the drainage should be good. The annual kinds are raised from seed sown in March in gentle heat and gradually hardened and planted in the border in late May to flower for the remainder of the season.

Twiggy stakes are needed for good effects, and bold planting repays in garden decoration. The perennial kinds prefer drier soils. Autumn and winter moisture is their enemy, and if they do not survive, it is probably because of dampness. On the other hand, a sun baked soil stunts the plants, so a mulch of leaf mold or decayed manure in summer is helpful. Liquid feeds can be given to good advantage when the plants are coming into flower. Cultivars are best propagated from root cuttings taken at any time between February and April and put in a sandy box in the frame or greenhouse. Those that are taken early and do well may flower the first year. Alternatively basal cuttings taken from August to October, put into a sandy soil in a cold frame will soon root. The plants can be divided in either October or March and any roots left in the ground at this time may sprout again.

Galega (gal-ee-ga)

From the Greek *gala*, milk, *ago,* to lead; the plant was used as fodder for cattle and goats and was thought to stimulate the flow of milk *(Leguminosae)*. Goat's rue. A small genus of hardy herbaceous plants with pinnate leaves, useful for the border. The only species likely to be found in cultivation is *G. officinalis,* 3—5 feet tall with spikes of bluish sweet pea shaped flowers in summer and autumn. It is variable in flower color and has several varieties, including *alba,* white flowers, and *hartlandii* with larger flowers of a better lilac than the type. Cultivars include 'Duchess of Bedford', mauve and white; 'Her Majesty', clear lilac; 'Lady Wilson', blue and white flushed with pink.

Cultivation In the border, put the galegas well to the back or towards the middle in an island border so that their tendency towards untidiness can be masked by other plants. Light twiggy stakes placed early in the season so that the leaf growth can hide the support and at the same time use it, are the best. Ordinary garden soil is all that is required and the plant does well on poor soils. It remains fairly compact, so does not

1 Gazania splendens is a showy flower.
2 The Gazania and its hybrids, such as the one shown here, are half hardy.

need dividing too often. Propagate by division of roots in October or March or from seed sown in April out of doors in a sunny position, thinned and later transplanted. Self sown seedlings usually appear in large numbers.

Gazania (gaz-ay-ne-a)

Commemorating Theodore of Gaza, fifteenth century translator of the botanical works of Theophrastus *(Compositae)*. Treasure flower. Half hardy perennials from South Africa, with showy flowers, which open in the sun and close about 3 p.m. The species hybridize freely and gazanias have been much improved in recent years; seed is offered in red and orange shades and pink and cream shades, both groups coming true from seed. The ray petals are frequently beautifully marked with zones of contrasting colors. All flower from June to September.

Species cultivated *G. longiscapa,* 6 inches, golden-yellow. *G. pavonia,* 1 foot yellow and brown. *G. rigens,* 1 foot, orange. *G. splendens,* 1 foot, orange, black and white. This, which is probably the showiest species, will thrive out of doors in very mild districts. Cultivars include 'Bridget', orange with black center; 'Freddie', yellow with green center; 'Roger', citron-yellow with a purple feathering at the center; 'Sunshine', deep yellow with a brown ring

Gentiana (jen-te-a-na)

Named after Gentius, King of Illyria who first used the plant medicinally (Gentianaceae). Gentian. A large genus of hardy perennials. Most of those in cultivation are dwarf plants suitable for the rock garden, but a few are more at home in the border.

Species cultivated G. acaulis (now considered to be a hybrid), gentianella, 4 inches, glossy green tufts of pointed leaves, stemless, deep blue trumpet flowers, spring; vars. alba, white; alpina, compact form; coelistina, pale blue; dinarica, short stemmed, clear blue flowers. G. angulosa, 2—5 inches, deep lilac, May and June. G. asclepiadea, 2—3 feet, willow gentian, dark blue flowers, July and August; var. alba, white. G. brachyphylla, 2 inches, deep blue flowers, spring. G. cachemirica, 4—6 inches, pale blue, August. G. clusii, 1—4 inches, deep blue, spring. G. dahurica, 6 inches, dark blue, August. G. farreri, 4 inches, Cambridge blue flowers, August and September. G. fetisowii, 6 inches, purplish-blue, August. G. gracilipes, 6 inches, deep blue, summer; var. alba, white. G. freyniana, 4 inches, pale blue, July to September. G. grombezewskii, 9 inches, pale yellow, August. G. hascombensis, 1 foot, blue, summer. G. × hexa-farreri, 3—4 inches, deep blue, August, hybrid. G. hexaphylla, 3 inches, pale blue flowers heavily marked on the outside with darker bars, July and August. G. × 'Inverleith', prostrate, clear blue, August and September, hybrid. G. lagodechiana, 9 inches, blue, white spotted, August and September. G. lutea, 4—6 feet, pale yellow in tall, unbranched spikes, June to August, bog garden. G. × macaulayi, 4 inches, deep blue, September and October, hybrid. G. pneumonanthe, 6—9 inches, heather gentian, bog gentian or marsh gentian, a native, deep blue, heavily speckled outside with bands of greenish spots, August and September; var. depressa, shorter, more prostrate; 'Styrian Blue' is upright (1½ feet) with larger, paler flowers. G. saxosa, 4 inches, ivory-white, summer. G. septemfida, 6—12 inches, bright blue, July. G. sino-ornata, 3 inches, deep blue, September. G. stragulata, 2—3 inches, deep purplish-blue, August. G. verna, 3 inches, deep blue, April and May.

Cultivation It is impossible to generalize about the cultivation of gentians. Some, such as G. cachemerica, hexa-farreri, hexaphylla, 'Inverleith', macaulayi, pneumonanthe, saxosa, sino-ornata and stragulata, will not tolerate lime. Most require a well drained, coarse soil containing leaf mold or peat, but both G. lutea and G. pneumonanthe are bog garden plants. These two, together with G. asclepiadea, will grow in partial shade. Others require sunny positions and although they like ample moisture in summer, they dislike winter moisture, hence the need for good drainage. All should be planted firmly. Propagation is by seed sown in March in a cold frame or in pans in a greenhouse. Seed sometimes takes a year or so to germinate

dotted white. In addition, under the name G. hybrida, seedsmen offer seed in mixed colors, including shades of yellow, pink, red, brown orange and white, variously marked.

Cultivation Treat the gazanias as half hardy annuals, sowing seed in gentle heat in February and hardening and planting out in May. They are not fussy about soil and will do well in alkaline soil, but must be given the sunniest possible positions. G. splendens can be propagated from cuttings in August, rooted in a cold frame. The rooted cuttings should be taken into a frost proof greenhouse for the winter un-

1 Gentiana acaulis has deep blue trumpet-shaped flowers in spring.
2 Gentiana lagodechiana flowers in late summer.
3 Gentiana sino-ornata is an effective bedding plant.

less the frame can be made frost proof. By potting these in spring, in a mixture of 2 parts of loam to 1 part of peat and 1 part of sand, as an alternative to planting them out of doors, they will make fine greenhouse flowering plants in early summer.

so the soil must be kept moist. *G. sino-ornata* and *G. acaulis* can be divided in spring, but many other species resent this kind of disturbance.

Geranium (jer-ay-ne-um)

From the Greek *geranos*, a crane, because the seed pod resembles a crane's head and beak (*Geraniaceae*). Crane's bill. A genus of hardy herbaceous summer flowering perennials with lobed or cut leaves, widely distributed over the temperate regions of the world. They are easily cultivated, free flowering, and some are useful rock garden plants, others good border plants. These should not be confused with common geranium, *pelargonium*, used as a pot plant or summer bedding plant.

Species cultivated *G. aconitifolium*, 15—18 inches, leaves finely divided, flowers white with black veins, May and June. *G. anemonifolium*, 1—2 feet, pale purple, May and June, may need winter protection. *G. argenteum*, 4 inches, clear pink, summer, scree plant. *G. atlanticum*, 9 inches, purple, red veined, summer. *G. can-*

True geraniums should not be confused with the Zonal Pelargoniums or Bedding Geraniums.

1 The summer flowering Geranium atlanticum grows to 9 inches in height.
2 The long lasting Geranium endressi blooms from June until October.
3 Geranium cinereum subcaulescens.

didum, 1 foot, spreading, sprawling habit, white, crimson centered, cup shaped flowers, summer. *G. celticum*, 4 inches, white, all summer. *G. cinereum*, 6 inches, pale pink, June to August; vars. *album*, white; *subcaulescens*, cerise, dark centered, May to October. *G. collinum*, 9—12 inches, red to purplish-violet, May and June. *G. dalmaticum*, 6—9 inches, pink, summer; var. *album*, white. *G. delavayi*, 1 foot, crimson, summer. *G. endressii*, 9—18 inches, light rose, June to October or later; cultivars include 'A. T. Johnson', silvery-pink; 'Rose Clair' salmon, veined purple; 'Wargrave Variety', deeper pink. *G. grandiflorum*, 1—1½ feet, blue, red veined, spring to autumn; var. *alpinum*, 9—12 inches, deeper

blue, larger flowered. *G. ibericum*, 1 foot, violet-purple, all summer. *G. kotschyi*, 9 inches, soft purple, darker veined, early summer. *G. macrorrhizum*, 18 inches, red to purple, all summer; var. *album*, white. 'Ingwersen's Variety', 9—12 inches, rose-pink, is a fine cultivar. *G. napuligerum* (syn. *G. farreri*), 4 inches, soft pink, May and June. *G. phaeum*, mourning widow, 18 inches, dark purple, May and June. *G. platypetalum*, 2 feet, deep violet, red veined, June and July. *G. pratense*, meadow crane's bill, 2 feet, blue, May to September; vars. *album*, white; *flore-pleno*, double blue; *roseum*, 1½ feet, rose-pink. *G. psilostemon* (syn. *G. armenum*), 2 feet, magenta-crimson, dark centered, May and June. *G. pylzowianum*, 3—4 inches, clear pink, early summer. *G. renardii*, 9 inches, white, purple centered, summer. *G. sanguineum*, bloody crane's bill, 6—24 inches, blood red, summer; vars. *album*, white; *lancastriense*, 4 inches, pink; *prostratum*, 6 inches, rosy-pink. *G. sessiliflorum*, prostrate, white and purple, summer; var. *nigricans*, dark leaves. *G. stapfianum* var. *roseum*, 4 inches, crimson-purple flowers,

45

flowers, summer. The species itself is rarely cultivated, but from it many cultivars, mostly with double flowers, have been produced. They include 'Dolly North', orange; 'Fire Opal', single orange overlaid with red; 'Lady Stratheden', golden-yellow; 'Prince of Orange', bright orange; 'Princess Juliana', golden-orange; 'Mrs Bradshaw', brilliant red; 'Red Wings', semi double, bright scarlet, late flowering. *G.* × *heldreichii* 9—12 inches, orange-red, summer, hybrid. *G. montanum,* 6—12 inches, yellow flowers, May. *G. reptans,* 6 inches, yellow, late summer. *G. rivale,* water avens, 1 foot, reddish, May and June, a native; 'Leonard's Variety', with pink and orange flowers, is a cultivar. *G. triflorum,* 9—12 inches, soft pink, July.

Cultivation Geums are easily grown in any good, well drained garden soil. They appreciate sunshine, but the border kinds are tolerant of shade and damp conditions. Propagation is by division in spring or autumn or from seed sown out of doors in April or May, or in a cold frame or greenhouse in March or April.

Gypsophila (jip-sof-ill-a)
From the Greek *gypsos,* chalk, *phileo,* to love; the plants prefer alkaline soils (*Caryophyllaceae*). Hardy annuals and perennials of great value in both the border and rock garden; the dwarf kinds also look well in pans in the alpine house. They are mainly natives of the eastern Mediterranean region.

Perennial species cultivated *G. aretioides,* 1 inch, a cushion plant for a sunny scree, with white, stemless flowers, spring. *G. cerastioides,* 3 inches, leaves in dense flat mats, white flowers much veined with purple, spring; var. *flore-pleno,* double flowers. There are various garden forms. *G. dubia,* mat like dark green foliage, white, pink flushed flowers, spring, good for walls or crevices. *G. pacifica* (syn. *G. oldhamiana*), 3—4 feet, dark leaves, pink flowers in cloudy sprays, August and September. *G. paniculata,* baby's breath, 2½—3 feet, light sprays of white flowers occasionally pinkish, June to August; vars. *compacta,* 1½ feet, *flore-pleno,* double flowers, a better form. Cultivars include 'Bristol Fairy', 3 feet, 'Rosy Veil' (sometimes called 'Rosenchleirer'), 9 inches, 'Flamingo', 2½ feet, large double pink flowers. *G. repens,* 6 inches, white flowers June to August; vars. *fratensis,* compact form, pink flowers. *rosea* 9 inches, rose-pink. 'Letchworth Rose', 9 inches, is a named cultivar.

Cultivation Plant both rock garden and border kinds in autumn or spring, the rock garden types in pockets containing a large amount of mortar rubble or limestone chippings. Although the border kinds like limy soil, they are tolerant of other soils but need a sunny spot with good drainage. They provide useful cut flower material when well grown. Propagation of the annual species and *G. repens* and *G. pacifica*

summer, richly colored autumn foliage. *G. striatum,* 15 inches, pale pink, reddish veins, May to October. *G. sylvaticum,* 18 inches, purple-blue, summer; vars. *album,* white; *roseum,* rose-pink. *G. tuberosum,* 9 inches, purplish, May; var. *charlesii,* pink. *G. wallichianum,* 1 foot, purple, August and September; 'Buxton's Blue', deep blue with a white eye, is the cultivar usually offered. *G. yunnanense,* 12—15 inches, white, purple veined, summer.

Cultivation In general the crane's bills are easy to grow, although, as noted above, some of the dwarf species need scree conditions in the rock garden. The others will grow in any kind of soil; most of them do best in a sunny position although *G. endressii,* one of the finest, as it produces its pink flowers over a very long period, will tolerate a good deal of shade, as will *G. aconitifolium, G. macrorrhizum* and *G. phaeum.* The taller species are apt to look a little untidy after they have flowered, and benefit from a trim just above the leaves to remove the spent flower stems. This will often result in a second flush of flowers being produced, especially if it is done before the seeds ripen. Most species form clumps (a few are tap-rooted) and these are very easily propagated by division in autumn or spring. With those that form vig-

Geum 'Lady Stratheden' is a popular double flowered cultivar which is a useful addition to the border.

orous, wide spreading clumps, such as *G. endressii* and *G. grandiflorum,* it is not even necessary to dig up the clumps in order to divide them; it is sufficient to cut away pieces from around the clump and replant these. Seeds may also be sown, either under glass in the cold frame or greenhouse, or out of doors, in March or April.

Geum (jee-um)
From the Greek *geno,* to impart an agreeable flavor, referring to the aromatic roots of some species (*Rosaceae*). Avens. A genus of hardy herbaceous perennials, some of which are useful border plants, the dwarf species are good rock garden plants. Several are natives of the British Isles but those valued for gardens are from Europe, South America and the Near East.

Species cultivated *G.* × *borisii,* 1 foot, vivid orange flowers, May to August, hybrid. *G. bulgaricum,* 1—1½ feet, yellow flowers, summer. *G. chiloense* (syn. *G. coccineum* in some catalogues), 2 feet, scarlet

is from seed. *G. paniculata* itself comes true from seed but cuttings of the varieties should be taken in June. These should be of young growth with a heel, 2 inches long, inserted in sand with gentle bottom heat. Commercially named forms are propagated by root grafting. Trailing species can be increased by cuttings or by division in spring.

Helenium (hel-ee-knee-um)

After Helen of Troy; according to legend the flowers sprang from her tears (*Compositae*). Sneezeweed. Hardy herbaceous perennials from North America, good for cutting and popularly grown for their late summer flowers. The disc of the flower head is very prominent, a characteristic of the entire genus.

Species cultivated *H. autumnale*, 3—5 feet, yellow flowers, July to October; var. *pumilum magnificum*, 3½ feet, golden-yellow. *H. bigelovii*, 4 feet, yellow and brown, July to September. *H. hoopesii*, 2 feet, yellow flowers, June onwards. There are many fine cultivars including 'Bruno', 3—3½ feet, bronze-red; 'Butterpat', 3—3½ feet, rich yellow. 'Chipperfield Orange', 4—5 feet, yellow streaked and splashed crimson; 'Copper Spray', 3½ feet, copper-red; 'Crimson Beauty', 2 feet, bronze-crimson; 'Goldlackzwerg', 2½—3 feet, gold and copper-red; 'July Sun', 3 feet, golden-bronze; 'Moerheim Beauty', 3—3½ feet, glowing bronze-red; 'Riverton Beauty', 4½ feet, yellow; 'Riverton Gem', 4½ feet, crimson steaked yellow; 'The Bishop', 3 feet, buttercup yellow; 'Wyndley', 2—2½ feet, chestnut and orange.

Cultivation Almost any garden soil is suitable, but a loam is ideal. Plant in autumn or spring, the lower growing types towards the front of the border in clumps and taller growing varieties towards the back. Propagate by division or by seed.

Helianthemum (hel-ee-an-them-um)

From the Greek *helios,* the sun, and *anthemon,* a flower (*Cistaceae*). Sun Rose. A genus of evergreen and semi evergreen shrubs, subshrubs, perennial plants and annuals, very free flowering. Numerous named varieties and hybrids are grown.

Species cultivated *H. alpestre*, 1 foot, a tufted alpine, yellow flowers, summer, European alps. *H. apenninum*, 1 foot, spreading plant, gray leaves, white flowers, June, short lived subshrub, Europe, southwest England and Asia Minor. *H.*

1 Gypsophila paniculata flore-pleno is the double flowered form.
2 The yellow-orange Helenium 'Wyndley' combines well with crimson 'Moerheim Beauty'.

lunulatum, 6—9 inches, subshrub, yellow, summer, Italy. *H. nummularium* (syn. *H. vulgare, H. chamaecistus*), common sun rose, 6—12 inches trailing, yellow, June, July, Europe (including England). There are many cultivars including 'Beech Park Scarlet', 'Ben Attow', primrose yellow, deeper center; 'Ben Hope', carmine shading to orange; 'Ben Ledi', dark red; 'Butterball', clear yellow, double; 'Jubilee', double yellow; 'Lemon Queen', lemon yellow; 'Mrs. C. W. Earle', scarlet, double; 'Rose of Leeswood', rich pink, large double; 'The Bride', white; 'Watergate Rose', deep carmine, foliage gray-green; 'Wisley Pink', clear pink. *H. tuberaria*, 9 inches, herbaceous perennial forming tufts of brownish leaves with yellow flowers, July, south Europe.

Cultivation As the name implies, a sunny spot is essential for the sun roses. Ordinary soil is suitable and they are excellent plants for dry walls, rock gardens and sunny banks. Most are not very long lived and need replacing in preference to cutting hard back to encourage new growth. Propagate from cuttings of young shoots in July or August, inserted in sandy soil. Once these are rooted they should be potted singly into small pots and over wintered thus. Because they do not transplant well, it is common practice to put them into their permanent positions from these pots, planting out in April.

Helianthus (hel-ee-an-thus)

From the Greek *helios,* the sun, *anthos,* a flower. (*Compositae*). Sunflower. A genus of tall, coarse growing plants, annuals and perennials, gross feeders which dominate the border in which they are planted. *H. annuus,* the common annual sunflower, is a plant of some economic importance, as the seeds are used in chicken and bird feeds, produce an edible oil, and the flowers yield a yellow dye.

Perennial species cultivated H *atrorubens* (syn. *H. sparsifolius*), 6—8 feet, golden-yellow, September, 'The Monarch', with flowers 6 inches across is a good cultivar. *H. decapetalus,* 4—6 feet, tough, sharply toothed leaves, sulphur yellow flowers, August to October. Cultivars include 'Capenoch Star', lemon yellow, single, good for cutting; 'Capenoch Supreme', large, single, pure yellow; 'Loddon Gold', double, rich yellow; 'Soleil d'Or', double, sulphur yellow, quilled petals. *H. laetiflorus* (syn. *H. rigidus*), 5—7 feet, yellow, September and October. 'Miss Mellish', orange-yellow, is the best cultivar of this, but both are very rampant plants. *H. salicifolius* (syn. *H. orgyalis*), 6 feet, small yellow flowers. September and October, willow like leaves. *H. tuberosus,* Jerusalem artichoke, 6—8 feet, yellow, October.

Cultivation The best plants are grown in loam in full sun. Seeds of annuals can be sown *in situ* in April or May. To get the largest flower heads, water and give liquid fertilizers occasionally up to flowering time. The perennials can be divided in autumn or spring. *H. laetiflorus* needs constant checking to prevent it from dominating the surrounding area and is best planted in rough corners where it will provide useful flowers for cutting.

Helichrysum (hel-ee-kry-sum)

From the Greek *helios,* the sun, *chrysos,* gold, referring to the yellow flowers of some species. (*Compositae*). Everlasting flower, Immortelle flower. A large genus of plants ranging from alpines to shrubs, bearing daisy like flowers. Some are commonly dried as everlasting flowers. Not all are hardy.

Perennial species cultivated *H. arenarium,* yellow everlasting 6—12 inches, bright yellow bracts, summer, Europe. *H. frigidum,* mat forming, silvery leaves, rather moss like, white flowers, May and June, suitable for scree or alpine house, Corsica. *H. marginatum* (syn. *H. milfordae*), 3 inches, forming hummocks of silvery rosettes, white, spring. *H. orientale,* 9 inches, yellow, August, southeast

Europe. *H. plicatum,* 1—3½ feet, silvery foliage, small yellow flowers, needs warm position, southeast Europe. Shrubby and subshrubby H. angustifolium, 1 foot, yellow, summer, southern Europe. *H. bellidoides,* mat forming, white flowers, summer, useful rock garden plant, New Zealand. *H. fontanesii,* 1 foot, narrow, silvery leaves, yellow flowers in loose sprays, summer, rock garden. *H. lanatum,* 1 foot, leaves white of a flannel like texture, yellow flowers, summer, useful for bedding, South Africa. *H. petiolatum,* 12—15 inches, white, summer. *H. rosmarinifolium* (syn. *Ozothamnus rosmarinifolius*), 6—9 feet, branches and leaves sticky, flowers white, small, produced very freely, June, Tasmania; var. *purpurescens,* 4 feet, purple. *H. selago,* 9 inches, white, summer, New Zealand. *H. splendidum,* 2—5 feet, shoots and leaves gray-white, flowers bright yellow, summer, South Africa. *H. stoechas,* goldilocks, 1—2 feet, leaves silvery-white, flowers yellow in heads to 2 inches across, summer, southern Europe. *H. virgineum,* 9 inches, cream, summer.

Cultivation Treat the annuals as half-hardy, sowing in gentle heat in March, gradually hardening and planting out in May. Late sowings can be made out of doors in early May. The rock garden kinds all like dry sunny, spots with sharp drainage, and make good scree plants. The shrubby

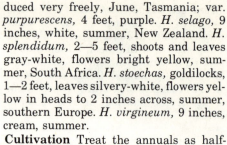

1 Helianthus 'Color Fashion' is a cultivar with enormous blooms.
2 Helianthus 'Italian White' is a single flowered form with white flowers and a yellow central zone.
3 Helichrysum virgineum has papery yellow flowers in summer.

kinds are rather tender and need protection in all except mild localities. Plant in April and fasten the main branches to a trellis or wire support. Prune away unwanted branches early in April. They may be grown as attractive greenhouse shrubs in a mixture of sand, peat and loam. Propagation of the perennial species is by division in April or by cuttings in a cold frame in spring, and of the shrubby kinds from cuttings of half ripened wood in August, inserted around the edges of a pot of sandy soil and put in a cold frame.

Heliopsis (he-le-op-sis)
From the Greek *helios,* the sun, *opsis,* like, referring to the flowers (*Compositae*). Orange sunflower. Hardy herbaceous perennials resembling sunflowers, good border plants, especially since the more recent introduction of several good forms; useful for cutting from July onwards.
Species cultivated *H. helianthoides* (syn. *H. laevis*), North American ox eye, 3—6 feet, rich yellow flowers. *H. scabra,* 3—4 feet, golden-yellow flowers; vars. *incomparabilis,* 3 feet, rich orange-yellow, semi double; *patula,* 3½ feet, large flowered semi double, golden-orange; *zinniiflora,* 2½ feet, orange, double, zinnia like flowers. *H. vitellina,* 3 feet, double golden-yellow. Cultivars include 'Golden Plume', double; 'Gold-greenheart', double, yellow with greenish center; 'Light of Loddon', branched growth, single, butter yellow flowers; 'Orange King', bright orange; 'Sonnenschild', 4 feet, golden-yellow; 'Summer Sun', clear orange-yellow.
Cultivation Plant in autumn or spring in sunny well drained borders but never let

1 *Heliopsis 'Light of Loddon' is an anemone centered Sunflower, butter yellow in color and double.*
2 *Heliopsis 'Golden Plume' is a fully double cultivar with long lasting flowers of bright gold.*

the plants suffer from drought. An occasional liquid fertilizer when the buds are swelling will help, or a mulch of leaf mold in May once the soil has warmed up is advantageous. Propagation is by division in spring.

Helleborus (hel-le-bor-us)
From the Greek *helein,* to kill, *bora,* food; some species are poisonous (*Ranunculaceae*). Hellebore. Hardy perennials, often retaining their leaves through the winter, with thick, fibrous roots. All flower early in the year and the flowers are long lasting. Most of them have handsome, leathery, divided leaves, sometimes spiny. They are natives of southern Europe and western Asia.
Species cultivated *H. abchasicus,* 1 foot, flowers purplish-green, January to March; vars. *coccineus,* wine red, *venousus,* rosy-purple with dark veins. *H. argutifolius* (syn. *H. corsicus*), 2—3 feet, apple-green flowers in February and March which persist until midsummer. *H. foetidus,* stinking hellebore, 2—3 feet, pale green flowers, the petals tipped purple, February and March, native plant. *H. guttatus,* 1½ feet, white flowers, heavily spotted with crimson inside, January to April, the parent of most spotted hybrids in cultivation. *H. lividus,* 3 feet, green flowers soon turning brown; doubtfully hardy. *H. niger,* 1½—2 feet; Christmas rose, 1 foot, white, saucer-

3 *Helleborus x nigricors, a pale green hybrid, is slightly perfumed.*
4 *Helleborus niger is the well loved Christmas Rose.*

shaped flowers with golden-yellow anthers; vars. *altifolius* and *macranthus*, longer stems. 'Potters Wheel' is a fine cultivar. *H. × nigricors*, (*H. niger × H. corsicus*), 1½ feet, pale green, February, hybrid. *H. odorus*, fragrant hellebore, 1½ feet, greenish-yellow flowers with faint elderflower scent, March. *H. orientalis*, Lenten rose, 2 feet, variable flowers, purple, pink or almost black and often spotted with other shades, February to May. 'Albion Otto' is a white, purple spotted cultivar. *H. torquatus*, 1½ feet, flowers purple inside and blue-purple outside, February to March, rather shy flowering, leaves die down in summer. *H. viridis*, green hellebore, 1—1½ feet, pale green flowers, February.

Cultivation A well drained, rich soil is best and although a shaded position is usually recommended, this is not essential, although partial shade is preferable to full sun. Once established, the plants like to be left undisturbed, although they quickly settle down if they are moved in winter with plenty of soil around their roots. In December, protect the flowers of the Christmas rose by a glass or plastic cover or by mulching with peat to prevent the short stemmed flowers from being splashed by soil. Plant in October or November, or March, 15 inches apart in groups, preparing the site well and incorporating some manure.

Plants can be forced in pots by lifting and potting up in October and maintaining a temperature of 40—50°F. Replant out of doors in April.

Propagate from seed or by division of roots after flowering.

Helxine (helks-in-e)
Derivation uncertain. Possibly from the ancient Greek name for pellitory, a related plant, or from the Latin *helix*, ivy, since the plant creeps (*Urticaceae*). Baby's tears. A genus of a single species from Corsica, *H. soleirolii*, a nearly hardy creeping perennial with insignificant flowers, grown for its attractive tiny, bright green leaves. It is quick growing and useful for dry walls and among paving stones in mild districts; it can become invasive but is blackened by frost; however, usually not all the plant is killed. It is particularly useful in cold greenhouses as an edging to benches or in pots or hanging baskets for conservatories. The plant grows about 2—3 inches tall. The varieties 'Silver Queen', with silver variegated foliage, and 'Golden Queen', with yellow variegation, are also attractive.

Cultivation Ordinary garden soil to which a little leaf mold has been added at planting time is suitable. Dry banks, rock work, dry walls in sun or shade are all suitable positions. It makes a good pot plant for patios, conservatories or cold greenhouses in a compost of 1 part of loam and 1 part of leaf mold. Pot in spring and water moderately. Propagation is easy by division in spring.

Hemerocallis (hem-er-o-kal-lis)
From the Greek *hemero*, a day, and *kallos*, beauty, referring to the life of the flowers (*Liliaceae*). Day lily. Hardy perennials from temperate E. Asia and S. Europe, very adaptable, flowering for many weeks, but with the individual funnel shaped flowers lasting only for one day. There have been a bewildering number of cultivars both from America and from England and continental Europe with the result that the species have been somewhat neglected.

Species cultivated *H. aurantiaca*, Japanese day lily, 3 feet, orange-yellow flowers, July. *H. citrina*, 3½ feet, lemon yellow, slightly fragrant flowers, July to September; var. *baronii*, larger flowers, citron yellow. *H. flava*, 2—3 feet, orange-yellow flowers, June and July. *H. fulva*, 3 feet, vigorous, orange-brown, June to August; vars. *flore pleno*, double, *kwanso flore pleno*, double flowers and variegated striped foliage. *H. × luteola*, 3 feet, large, light yellow, June and July, hybrid. *H. middendorffi*, 1—1½ feet, rich yellow, fragrant, June. *H. minor*, 9 inches, clear yellow, reddish-brown on outside, June. *H. thunbergii*, 2—3 feet, light yellow, fragrant, July to September. There are many

1 Hemerocallis 'Orange Beauty' has clear bright yellow flowers.
2 Hemerocallis 'Black Prince' is a striking Day Lily.

1

2

cultivars such as 'Ambassador', currant red, rich yellow center; 'Apollo' bright apricot yellow; 'Bagette', dark brown; 'Ballet Dancer', soft pink; 'Black Prince', purple-red; 'Bonanza', soft golden-yellow, dwarf; 'Display', bright red; 'Golden Chimes', golden-yellow, a miniature with well branched growth; 'Hyperion', canary yellow; 'Morocco Beauty', very dark purple with golden throat; 'Norma Borland', copper; 'Pink Prelude', flesh pink, yellow throat; 'Rajah', late flowering, orange, shaded mahogany and violet; 'Red Torch', cardinal red; 'Viscountess Byng', orange flushed rose, long flowering season. New ones appear each year; nurserymen's catalogues should be consulted for the latest varieties.

Cultivation Day lilies are most accommodating as to soil and position, provided they are not planted in full shade. They do not, however, give of their best in poor, limestone soils. Plant in autumn or spring, incorporating some compost. The plants will survive for many years, unattended except for an occasional early summer mulch and a regular dressing of slug repellent.

Hepatica (he-pat-ik-a)

From the Greek *hepar*, liver, from a supposed resemblance of the leaves to that organ (*Ranunculaceae*). A genus of three or four species of low growing hardy perennials, sometimes included in the genus

1 Hemerocallis fulva 'Kwanso' is a double flowered Day Lily with orange blooms.
2 Heracleum villosum is a coarse growing plant for the wild garden.
3 Hesperis matronalis, the Sweet Rocket or Dame's Violet, bears fragrant white to pale lilac blooms in early summer.

Anemone and growing wild in woodlands over the whole of the north temperate zone.
Species cultivated *H. americana* (syns. *H. triloba, Anemone hepatica*), 6 inches, almost stemless deep lavender-blue flowers, March; vars. *alba*, white, *rubra flore pleno*, double pink. *H. media*, 9 inches, offered in its var. *ballardii*, large clear blue flowers, spring. *H. transsilvanica* (syns. *Anemone transsilvanica, A. angulosa*), 3—5 inches, lavender-blue, slightly larger flowers than *H. americana*, spring. A pink form is sometimes offered.
Cultivation The leaves appear after the flowers and form good green tufts for the remainder of the summer and throughout the winter. Shady rock gardens or shrub borders in moist soil suit them best. Propagation is from seed sown in pans of sandy compost in autumn or by division of the roots.

Heracleum (her-ak-le-um)

Named after Hercules who is said to have discovered the plant's medicinal uses, or after *heracles*, a plant dedicated to Her-

cules (*Umbelliferae*). Cow parsnip. Vigorous and coarse growing hardy perennials suitable for the wilder parts of the garden.
Species cultivated *H. mantegazzianum,* 7—9 feet, small white flowers in summer carried on enormous umbels, up to 4½ feet across, stems coarse and thick, ridged and bearing very large leaves, individually about 3 feet long, together making a tuft 10—12 feet across. *H. villosum* (syn. *H. giganteum*), cartwheel flower, 10—14 feet, white flowers carried in great flattened umbels, rough stout stems and enormous deeply cut leaves.
Cultivation These plants thrive in any soil, but attain their best proportions in deeply dug, manured ground. Plant in the autumn in the wild garden or on the margins of lakes and streams. If they are required for foliage effect, remove the flowering shoots once they appear in June because better foliage is produced if the plant is prevented from flowering. Propagation is from seed sown in March out of doors or from division of established plants in either October or March.

Hesperis (hes-per-is)
From the Greek *hesperos,* evening, when the flowers of some species become fragrant (*Cruciferae*). A genus of hardy plants including biennial and perennial species. Similar in form to *Matthiola* and *Cheiranthus,* and native to Europe and W. and N. Asia.

Perennial species cultivated *H. matronalis,* sweet rocket, dame's violet, dame's rocket, 2—3 feet, flowers fragrant in evenings, variable between white and lilac, May to July; vars. *candissima,* 15 inches, pure white, *purpurea,* purple. Double forms have appeared from time to time but are rare in cultivation.
Biennial *H. tristis,* 1—2 feet, flowers ranging from white through brick red to purple, fragrant at night, summer. *H. violacea,* 6—12 inches, violet flowers, June.
Cultivation *H. matronalis* and its forms will thrive in an ordinary soil with a regular moisture supply, in full sun. Plant in autumn or spring. Plants do best if mulched with well rotted manure in May. Remove spent flower stalks in autumn. Double types, when obtainable, benefit from occasional extra feeding with liquid fertilizer during summer, and replanting in alternate years. Single types can be raised from seed sown ¼ inch deep in a warm spot outside in April. Transplant seedlings in June or July. Double types can be perpetuated only by cuttings, 3 inches long, taken from July to September, and inserted in a shaded position outdoors.

1 Heuchera 'Scintillation' is a cultivar that provides color throughout the summer months.
2 The flowers of the half hardy greenhouse perennial Impatiens, Busy Lizzie or Balsam, are attractively marked.

Later cuttings, taken in September or October, require glass protection. Transplant in March. Established plants may be divided in autumn or spring. Biennial species are raised from seed sown direct in sunny flowering positions in July. Thin seedlings to 9 inches apart. *H. violacea* can be established on stone walls where a root hold permits.

Heuchera (hu-ker-a)
Named in honor of Professor J. H. Heucher, 1677-1747, German professor of medicine, and a botanist (*Saxifragaceae*). Alum root. A genus of hardy perennials with dainty, small, bell like flowers in loose panicles which are produced over a long period, blooming on and off from spring through to autumn. The leaves are evergreen and the flowers are attractive when cut for indoor use.
Species cultivated *H. americana,* 18 inches, red flowers, summer. *H. × brizoides,* 1 foot, pink flowers, hybrid. This name includes various hybrids, such as 'Coral Cloud', produced by crossing *H. americana* with *H. sanguinea. H. micrantha,* 2 feet, pale yellow flowers, summer. *H. pubescens,* 1 foot, flowers deep pink marked with yellow, summer, foliage mottled with brown. *H. sanguinea,* coral bells, 12—18 inches, red flowers, summer; vars. include *alba,* white, *atrosanguinea,* deep red, *grandiflora,* large flowers, coral scarlet; *rosea,* rose-red; *splendens,* dark

crimson. *H. villosa,* 1—3 feet, small pink flowers, late summer. Cultivars include 'Bressingham Blaze', 2 feet, coral flame; 'Bressingham Hybrids' a fine modern strain with flowers from crimson to pink in all shades. 'Carmen', 2 feet, intense carmine-pink; 'Edge Hall', 2 feet, bright rose; 'Oakington Jewel', 2½ feet, deep coral rose, coppery tinge; 'Pearl Drops', 2 feet, white; 'Pluie de Feu', 1½ feet, bright red; 'Red Spangles', 20 inches, crimson scarlet; 'Rhapsody', 20 inches, glowing pink; 'Scintillation', 2 feet, bright pink, tipped carmine; 'Snowflake', 2 feet, white; 'Sparkler', 2 feet, carmine and scarlet; 'Splendour', 2½ feet, salmon-scarlet.

Cultivation Heucheras do best in light but rich, well drained soil or in ordinary soil with peat added in full sun or partial shade. Plants do not thrive in clay. Plant in autumn or spring. Increase by dividing plants from March to May or by sowing seeds in spring under glass protection in a light compost. Seedlings are best grown in pots for planting out when a year old.

Impatiens (im-pa-she-ens)

From the Latin *impatiens* in reference to the way the seed pods of some species burst and scatter their seed when touched (*Balsaminaceae*). Balsam, busy lizzie. A genus of about 500 species of annuals, biennials and subshrubs mostly from the mountains of Asia and Africa. The succulent hollow stems are brittle and much branched. Few

Incarvillea delavayi is an early summer flowering herbaceous perennial.

species are now cultivated; those that are may be grown in flower borders or under glass, or as house plants.

Species cultivated *I. balsamina,* 1½ feet, rose, scarlet and white, summer, annual greenhouse. *I. holstii,* 2—3 feet, scarlet, almost continuous flowering, half hardy, greenhouse perennial; var. Imp Series, F₁, low growing, brilliant mixed colors, in shade and sun. *I. petersiana,* 1 foot, reddish-bronze leaves and stems, red, almost continuous flowering, half hardy, greenhouse perennial. *I. sultanii,* 1—2 feet, rose and carmine, almost continuous flowering, greenhouse perennial. *I. amphorata,* 5 feet, purple, August, annual. *I. roylei* (syn. *I. glandulifera*), 5 feet, purple or rose-crimson, spotted flowers in profusion, summer, annual.

Cultivation Greenhouse plants are potted in a mixture of equal parts loam, leaf mold and sharp sand in well drained pots, during February or March. They do best in well lighted conditions and require moderate watering March—September, but only occasionally otherwise. They require a temperature of 55—65°F from October to March, 65—75°F March to June, and about 65°F for the rest of the time. Pinch back the tips to make them bushy during February. Hardy species do well in ordinary soil in a sunny position, about 6 inches apart. *I. holstii* can be grown as a

bedding plant and prefers light shade out of doors; it will tolerate varied temperatures. Propagate by seed in spring, sown in heat for the greenhouse species, and out of doors where the plants are to grow for the hardy species, or by cuttings taken March to August, and placed in sandy soil at a temperature of 75°F.

Incarvillea (in-kar-vil-le-a)

Commemorating Pierre d'Incarville (1706-57), a French Jesuit missionary to China (*Bignoniaceae*). A genus of about 6 species of herbaceous perennials, first introduced in the mid nineteenth century, hardy or nearly hardy in suitable conditions.

Species cultivated *I. delavayi,* 2 feet, rose-pink trumpet shaped flowers in May and June. *I. grandiflora,* 1½ feet, large, deep rose-red flowers with orange tube, and throat blotched white, June—July; var. *brevipes,* a variety with crimson flowers. *I. olgae,* 2—3 feet, somewhat shrubby, with clusters of pale pink flowers and finely divided foliage, summer.

Cultivation A light, well drained warm soil in a sunny but sheltered border is essential. Cold, with standing water is fatal. Plant in March or April, and protect the crowns in winter. Liquid fertilizers applied occasionally during the summer are beneficial. Propagation is by division of large plants in autumn or by seed in March, or in a cold frame in April, transplanting outdoors in June. Seedlings may take 3 years to reach flowering size.

Iris (eye-ris)

From the Greek *iris,* a rainbow (*Iridaceae*), A large genus of bulbous, creeping and tuberous rooted perennials, some of which are evergreen. They are natives of the north temperate zone from Portugal to Japan. Among the most varied and beautiful of flowers, irises have been compared to orchids by some gardeners who, without the required greenhouse facilities for orchids, have decided to specialize in this most interesting genus. They may be divided into six main groups: tall bearded, dwarf bearded, beardless, Japanese, cushion or regelia and bulbous rooted.

Tall bearded These are known best as the flag or German irises, flowering in May and June, and suitable for growing in ordinary, well drained borders, especially on limestone. *I. flavescens,* 2½ feet, pale lemon flowers, almost white, probably of garden origin. *I. florentina,* 2½ feet, white flowers tinged pale blue on the falls, May; grown near Florence for orris root. This iris is the fleur-de-lis of French heraldry. *I. germanica,* common iris, 2—3 feet, lilac-purple flowers, May. Other forms slightly differently colored.

Dwarf bearded Growing requirements similar to those of the previous group. *I. chamaeiris* (syn. *I. lutescens*), 10 inches, blue, purple, yellow or white, tinged and veined brown, April—May, S. Europe.

Most variable in color and growth, and frequently confused with *I. pumila*. *I. pseudopumila,* 6—9 inches, purple, yellow or white, April, southern Italy. *I. pumila,* 4—5 inches, almost stemless and much variation in color, April, Europe, Asia Minor.

Beardless Species suitable for moist soils, margins of pools or streams. *I. douglasiana,* 6—12 inches, variable in color, violet, reddish-purple, buff, yellow white, May, leaves evergreen and leathery, California. *I. fulva* (syn. *I. cuprea*), 2—3 feet, bright reddish-brown, June—July, southern United States; var. *violacea* is a violet form. *I. foetidissima,* gladwyn iris, 2 feet, lilac-blue flowers followed by an ornamental seed capsule with breaks to expose brilliant orange seeds in winter, Britain. *I. ochroleuca,* 4—5 feet, creamy-white, with orange blotch, June—July, western Asia Minor. *I. pseudacorus,* yellow flag or water flag, 2—3 feet, bright orange-yellow, May—June, Europe; *variegata,* with variegated leaves. *I. sibirica,* 2—3 feet, blue, purple, gray or occasionally white, June—July, invaluable for waterside or border planting, central Europe and Russia. *I. versicolor,* 2 feet, claret purple, May—June, N. America.

Species requiring sunny exposure: *I. chrysographes,* 1½ feet, deep violet with golden veins, for a moist place, June, Yunnan. *I. innominata,* 4—6 inches, golden-buff, veined light brown, and there are lavender, apricot and orange-yellow forms, Oregon; 'Golden River' is an attractive named cultivar. *I. japonica* (syn. *I. fimbriata*), 1—1½ feet, lilac, spotted yellow and white, evergreen, sage green leaves, April, Japan, China. The form 'Ledger's Variety' is said to be hardier than the type. *I. tectorum,* 1—1½ feet, bright lilac, flecked and mottled with deeper shades. There is a white form. Lift and divide after second year's flowering, May—June, Japan. *I. unguicularis* (syn. *I. stylosa*), 1 foot, lavender, blue, November—March, ideal in dry poor

1 The blue flowered Iris unguicularis blooms in winter or early spring in mild climates.
2 Iris douglasiana produces flowers in a wide range of colors.
3 Iris laevigata flowers in summer.
4 Iris xiphium is the Spanish Iris.
5 Iris longipetala.
6 Iris danfordiae
7 Iris histroides.
8 The deep blue form of Iris reticulata.
9 Divide clumps of Iris after they flower.
10 Cut the leaves back to about 9 inches, making 'fans'.
11 Set the plant into a hole, leaving the rhizome above ground to get the light.

marked cobalt-blue and whitish veins. For a sunny position, April, Turkestan. *I. histrioides,* short, dark blue, purple, January, Asia Minor. *I. reticulata,* 6 inches, violet, purple and yellow, February, Caucasus. *I. winogradowii,* 3—4 inches, light yellow, January—February, Caucasus. *I. xiphioides,* English iris, 1—2 feet, various colors, June—July, Pyrenees. *I. xiphium,* Spanish iris, 1—2 feet, various colors, white, yellow or blue, with orange patch on blade, May—June, south Europe and North Africa.

Miscellaneous *I. cristata,* 4—6 inches, pale lilac with deep yellow crest. A delightful miniature for a sink garden in full sun, May—June, eastern United States. *I. vicaria* (syn. *I. magnifica*), 2 feet, white, tinged pale blue, April, central Asia. Other species are offered.

Cultivation The most widely grown of this large and varied family are the tall bearded irises. These colorful hybrids have been developed by plant breeders from the long cultivated, dark blue *Iris germanica.* This type of iris is one of the few plants that may be lifted, divided and replanted soon after it has finished flowering, preferably in July. The fleshy rhizomes will soon make new roots in the warm soil and will be firmly established before the winter.

Choose a sunny well drained site, and if planting in wet, heavy soil is unavoidable, build the bed up a few inches above the surrounding level. In light soil, add leaf mold or peat, but manure should be used sparingly, for it will only induce soft growth. These irises like lime, so if the soil is deficient in this, work in some. It is important not to bury the rhizome when planting. In nature, it grows just under the surface of the soil, and if the rhizome is planted too deep a year's flowering may be lost. In light soil it is necessary to plant somewhat deeper, otherwise the plants are liable to topple over. It is usual at planting time to cut back the sword like leaves, but this can be overdone, for the plants do depend, to some extent, on the leaves to assist them in making new roots; drastic cutting back should be avoided. When planting, leave ample room so the rhizomes will not require lifting and dividing for three years.

For those who do not know one cultivar from another the best way to start a collection is to buy 12 cultivars in 12 different shades of color from an iris specialist nursery. With several hundred different named cultivars listed in iris catalogues it will be an easy matter to obtain individual cultivars to increase the selection. Among outstanding modern hybrids are: 'Berkeley Gold', a handsome tall deep gold; 'Blue Shimmer', ivory-white dotted with clear blue; 'Caprilla', yellow-bronze falls and blue-lavender standards; 'Chivalry', a ruffled medium blue; 'Cliffs of Dover', creamy-white; 'Dancer's Vale', with pale violet dottings on a white ground; 'Desert Song', a ruffled cream and primrose; 'Enchanter's Violet', violet; 'Golden Alps', white and yellow; 'Green Spot'; 'Harriet

soil. One of the gems of winter. Japanese: These species thrive in 2—4 inches of water and do well in moist soil or on the margins of ponds. *I. kaempferi,* Japanese iris, 2 feet, varying shades lilac, pink, blue and white, June and July. *I. laevigata,* 2 feet, deep blue, June and July.

Cushion or Regelia Very beautiful, easily grown hardy irises, doing best in a calcareous soil in a sunny sheltered site. *I. hoogiana,* 1½—2 feet, soft lavender-blue flowers, early May, Turkestan. *I. korolkowii,* 1—1½ feet, chocolate-brown markings on creamy-white ground, May, Turkestan.

Bulbous rooted Other than the Spanish and English iris which may be planted in sunny borders, this group includes choice kinds which may be grown in pots in the alpine house or in the rock garden. *I. bucharica,* 1—1½ feet, golden-yellow falls and small white standards, April, Bokhara. *I. bakeriana,* 4—6 inches, deep violet, with a touch of yellow on the falls, January-February, Asia Minor. *I. danfordiae,* short, bright yellow, January and February. A gem but rarely survives to flower a second year. *I. filifolia,* 1—1½ feet, deep purple, June, southern Spain. *I. graeberiana,* 6—8 inches, mauve falls

Thoreau', a large orchid-pink self; 'Inca Chief', a ruffled bronze-gold; 'Jane Phillips', intense pale blue; 'Kangchenjunga', pure white; 'New Snow', pure white with bright yellow beard; 'Pegasus', a tall white; 'Party Dress', a ruffled flamingo pink; 'Patterdale', a clear pale blue; 'Regal Gold', glowing yellow; 'South Pacific', a pale shimmering blue; 'Total Eclipse', almost black with a similar colored beard, and many Benton hybrids.

Waterside irises are charming beside a formal pool or in a wild garden. The June flowering *I. sibirica* and its hybrids have long been appreciated. They thrive in boggy conditions, although they will grow in a border provided the soil is deeply dug, reasonably moist and in partial shade. In the bog garden they flower well in full sun. Good hybrids include: 'Heavenly Blue', 'Perry's Blue' with china blue flowers on 3 foot stems, and 'Eric the Red' with heavily veined wine red flowers. The elegant *I. kaempferi*, of Japanese origin, is in all its glory in June or July. The flowers are large and handsome, with blends of color of great charm. There are both single and double types in shades of velvety purple, rosy-lilac, plum and white shaded blue, for instance, 'Morning Mist', purple, flecked gray, and a double white, 'Moonlight Waves'. They must have acid soil and, for that matter, alkali free water. They like a rich loam with ample moisture during the growing season but moderately dry roots during the rest of the year. Another handsome Japanese species, *I. laevigata*, is sometimes confused with the Japanese Iris *I. kaempferi*. The large, brilliant, violet-blue flowers of *I. laevigata* are borne on 2 foot stems at intervals from June to September, above a mass of deep green, arching foliage. It does well in a bog garden or in water up to 4 inches deep. The North American, claret colored water flag, *I. versicolor,* is also a good waterside plant.

1 *Iris 'Caprilla'.*
2 *Iris 'Regal Gold'.*
3 *Iris 'Jane Phillips'.*
4 *Japanese Iris kaempferi.*
5 *Iris 'Patterdale'.*
6 *Iris 'Pegasus'.*

These waterside irises are best propagated by division of the roots in the spring, although it can be done in the autumn if necessary. They may also be raised from seed sown in a cold frame in the autumn in well drained soil, covering them with ½ an inch of sifted soil. They should germinate in the spring, but some may prove erratic, so do not discard the seed pots too soon.

The bulbous irises are quite distinct from the tall bearded and waterside irises. They are admirable for the rock garden or in a sunny well drained border containing plenty of sharp sand or grit. Plant the bulbs in September. The miniature varieties which flower in February and March may also be grown in pans in a cold greenhouse or frame—the violet-blue *I. reticulata*, and its pale blue variety 'Cantab', *I. histrioides major,* bright blue with yellow markings, and bright yellow *I. danfordiae,* are particularly suitable for this purpose. The taller growing Dutch, Spanish and English irises are easily grown in any reasonably good soil in the garden and are most useful for cutting. Plant the bulbs in October about 4 inches deep in a sunny position.

1

2

3

4

5

6

The Dutch irises produced by crossing *I. xiphium* with other bulbous species, flower in June, followed a little later by the Spanish and then English. The English irises prefer a cool moist position and should be left undisturbed for three or four years before being lifted and divided. Dutch and Spanish irises should be lifted every year after the foliage has died down, and stored until planting time. There is a good selection of named types in bulb catalogues.

By making a careful selection of the many different types of iris, including the April flowering Juno species and hybrids which have brittle, swollen roots needing careful handling, it is possible to have irises of one sort or another in flower for many months of the year.

Kniphofia (nif-of-e-a)

Commemorating a German professor of medicine, Johann Hieronymus Kniphof, 1704-63 (*Liliaceae*). Red hot pokers. These herbaceous perennials from South and East Africa and Madagascar are tolerant of wind, but dislike poorly drained soil. They are often seen in seaside gardens where the milder climate suits them well, as they are not altogether hardy and need protection in the winter in colder areas. There are many good garden hybrids and varieties of *K. uvaria* in colors ranging from pure yellow through to reds, some of them being shaded in the spikes. The leaves are strap shaped.

Species cultivated *K. caulescens*, 4 feet, buff changing to red, autumn. *K. foliosa*, 3 feet, yellow tinged with red, late summer. *K. galpinii*, 2—3 feet, slender plant, orange-red flowers, late autumn. *K. macowanii*, 2 feet, slender plant, orange-red late summer. *K. nelsonii*, 2 feet, bright scarlet tinged orange, autumn. *K. northiae*, 2 feet, foliage gray-green, flowers yellow at base changing to red up the spikes,

1 Kniphofia 'Springtime' is typical of the striking and attractive half hardy Red Hot Pokers.
2 Kniphofias are especially effective when grown in sturdy clumps in the late summer garden.
3 Kniphofia uvaria 'Buttercup' is a fine, hardy cultivar with yellow flower spikes reaching 3½ feet in height.

October. *K. pumila,* 4 feet, gray-green foliage, orange-red flowers, to orange-yellow and finally yellowish-green, August. *K. uvaria,* 4 feet, coral red, late summer. A hardy species from which many hybrids and cultivars have been developed; they include 'Buttercup', 3½ feet, yellow; × *erecta,* 4 feet, orange-scarlet; 'Maid of Orleans', 4 feet, ivory-white; 'Mount Etna', 5 feet, large terra-cotta spikes; 'Royal Standard', 3 feet, deep gold; 'Yellow Hammer', 3 feet, yellow to orange.

Cultivation Plant in autumn or spring, choosing an open sunny position. Divide the clumps in spring as it becomes necessary. Kniphofias prefer a rich soil. Propagate by seed, but seedlings will not reach flowering size for about three years and then may not breed true.

Lathyrus (lath-ear-rus)

Lathyrus is the ancient Greek name for the pea (*Leguminaceae*). A genus of hardy annual and herbaceous perennial climbers, from temperate zones and tropical mountains.

Perennial species cultivated *L. grandiflorus,* 5 feet, rosy carmine, summer, southern Europe. *L. latifolius,* 10 feet, everlasting pea, bright carmine, August; var. *albus,* white flowers. *L. magellanicus,* 8 feet, bluish-purple, summer to early autumn, Straits of Magellan. *L. pubescens,* 5 feet, pale blue, mid to late summer, Chile. *L. rotundifolius,* 6 feet, pink, summer, Asia Minor. *L. splendens,* subshrub, 1 foot, carmine, summer, California. *L. undulatus,* 3 feet, rosy-purple, early summer, Turkey. *L. vernus,* 1 foot, purple and blue, spring, Europe.

Cultivation Any good rich soil is suitable. Plant the perennials in the autumn or spring, choosing a sunny position where the plants can climb over a trellis, wall or other support. These plants need a lot of water in the growing season and they should be fed during the summer with liquid or a complete fertilizer. In the autumn cut the stems and top-dress with manure in the spring. The perennial species are propagated by seeds or by division of the roots in the spring.

Leptosyne (lep-to-sy-knee)

From the Greek *leptos,* slender, describing the growth of these plants (*Compositae*). A small genus of hardy annuals and perennials that deserve to be better known, as they are showy in the garden and good as cut flowers. They are very similar in appearance to *Coreopsis,* to which they are closely related, and are natives of America.

Species cultivated Annual: *L. calliopsidea,* 1½ feet, yellow, late summer. *L. douglasii,* 1 foot. *L. stillmanii,* 1½ feet,

bright yellow, autumn. Perennial: *L. maritima,* 1 foot, yellow, autumn.

Cultivation Any ordinary soil will suit these plants but they like an open, sunny position. Sow seeds of the annual species in the spring in the open ground where the plants are to flower, or sow them under glass and transplant the seedlings to their flowering positions in late May or early June. The perennial species can be planted in the autumn or spring and they are either raised from seed or from division of the plants in the autumn or spring. Cuttings of young growth can be taken and rooted in a frame.

Ligularia (li-gu-lair-ee-a)

From the Latin *ligula,* a strap, referring to the strap shaped ray florets (*Compositae*). A genus of about 80 species of herbaceous perennials, formerly included in *Senecio.*

1 Lathyrus latifolius, the Everlasting Pea, and 2 Lathyrus undulatus are both excellent perennial climbers.

These handsome members of the daisy family from the temperate zones of the Old World grow best in moist situations. In recent years they have been considerably hybridized and some striking varieties have been obtained.

Species cultivated *L. dentata* (syn. *L. clivorum*), 4—5 feet, orange-yellow, July—September, China; cultivars include 'Desdemona', large, heart shaped leaves with a purple tinge, orange flowers; 'Gregynog Gold', 4 feet, large rounded leaves, orange-yellow flowers in pyramidal spikes; 'Othello', leaves veined purple, and large orange flowers. *L. × hessei*, 5 feet, flowers orange, August—September. *L. hodgsonii*, 1½ feet, rounded leaves, orange-yellow flowers. *L. japonica*, 3—5 feet, orange-yellow flowers, July, Japan. *L. przewalskii*, 3—4 feet, stems purple tinged, deeply cut leaves, tapering spikes of small yellow flowers, June and July; 'The Rocket', 5 feet, orange, August, is a cultivar. *L. tussilaginea*, 1—2 feet, softly hairy stems, light yellow flowers, August, Japan. *L. veitchiana*, 4—6 feet, leaves large, roughly triangular, yellow flowers in long flat spikes, July and August. *L. wilsoniana*, 5—6 feet, similar to *L. veitchiana*, flower spikes more branched, June.

Cultivation These hardy perennials grow best in a good, loamy soil; if possible fairly moist. They do well in slight shade; otherwise any position will suit them. *L. japonica* and *L. dentata* are most successful at the edge of a pool or stream. Mulching occasionally with rotted garden compost or similar material is beneficial. They are propagated by dividing the crowns in autumn or spring, by taking cuttings in spring or by sowing seed in spring in the cold greenhouse or out of doors in early summer.

Limonium (li-mo-nee-um)

From the Greek *leimon*, a meadow, because certain species are found growing in salt marshes (*Plumbaginaceae*). Sea lavender. A genus of annuals, perennial herbaceous plants and subshrubs, hardy, half hardy and tender. Once known as *Statice*, these plants are natives of all parts of the world, particularly coasts and salt marshes. The numerous small flowers, usually borne in branched spikes, are easily dried and are much used for long lasting flower arrangements. All flower in summer.

Species cultivated Perennial: *L. altaicum*, 15 inches, blue. *L. bellidifolium*, 9 inches, white or blue, Europe including Britain. *L. dumosum*, 2 feet, silvery-gray. *L. incanum*, 1½ feet, crimson, Siberia; vars. *album*, dwarf, white; *nanum*, 6 inches, dwarf; *roseum*, 6 inches, rosy-pink. *L. latifolium*, 2—3 feet, blue, south Russia.

1 Ligularia przewalskii bears yellow flowered spikes with purplish stems and deeply cut leaves.
2 Limonium latifolium is the Sea Lavender.

Cultivation The flaxes are not fussy about soil, provided it is well-drained, and will do very well on an alkaline medium. Most of the perennials and shrubby species will thrive and certainly look well in the rock garden in full sun. *L. arboreum* is not entirely hardy. Propagate by seed sown in April outdoors, or by firm cuttings taken in summer and kept close until rooted.

Lobelia (lobe-ee-lee-a)

Commemorating Matthias de L'Obel, 1538-1616, a Fleming, botanist and physician to King James I (*Campanulaceae*). A genus of some 200 species of annuals, herbaceous perennials or subshrubs, widely distributed over temperate and tropical regions of the world. All should be regarded as half hardy, although the herbaceous perennials will survive out of doors in the milder parts of the temperate zone. Elsewhere, the bright red flowered species may well be grown in the garden from June onwards, but usually need protection in winter. These red flowered Lobelias have the additional charm of dark purple-bronze leaves.

Species cultivated *L. cardinalis,* cardinal flower, perennial, 3 feet, scarlet, late summer, North America, short lived; var. *alba,* white; 'Queen Victoria' is a cultivar with bronze foliage, deep scarlet flowers, *L. erinus,* annual, 6 inches, blue, summer, South Africa; cultivars include 'Blue Gown', dwarf, sky blue; 'Blue Stone', clear blue without eye; 'Crystal Palace', bronze foliage, intense blue flowers; 'Emperor William', compact, bright blue, very good for bedding; 'Prima Donna', wine; 'Rosamund', deep carmine-red with white eye. This is the lobelia much used for summer bedding. *L. fulgens,* perennial, 3 feet, scarlet, May—September, Mexico. *L.* × *gerarens,* perennial, 3—4 feet, pink to violet-purple, July, hybrid. *L. syphilitica,* perennial, 2 feet, blue, autumn, Eastern United States, hardy. *L. tenuior,* annual, 1 foot, blue, September, western Australia, the Lobelia of trailing habit, used for hanging baskets. *L. tupa,* perennial, 6—8 feet, reddish-scarlet, autumn.

Cultivation The scarlet flowered *L. cardinalis* and *L. fulgens* when planted in the border need frequent watering since in their native habitat they are stream side plants. They are otherwise not difficult to grow. In cold areas, mulch during winter. Propagation of these is by seeds, sown in sandy soil in autumn in a cold frame, or in a temperature of 55°F in March or by cuttings rooted in a warm propagating frame. Plants may also be divided in March. The bedding Lobelias with blue flowers may be grown from seed sown in February in the greenhouse, but in September these plants may be lifted and stored in the greenhouse to provide cuttings for rooting in a heated propagating frame in March.

L. minutum, 6 inches, violet, Mediterranean area. *L. peticulum,* 4 inches, white. *L. puberulum,* 6 inches, violet to white, hardy in milder areas only, Canaries. *L. sinense,* 1 foot, yellow, China. *L tataricum,* 1 foot, red and white, southeast Europe and Siberia. *L. vulgare,* 1 foot, purple-blue flowers, Europe including Britain.

Cultivation All the limoniums prefer well drained, sandy loam and a sunny position. The hardy species are suitable for borders, the dwarf kinds for rock gardens. Plant the hardy perennials in spring and the annuals in late May. Greenhouse species are potted in the spring and fed occasionally with a weak liquid fertilizer. They require a summer temperature of 55—65°F and 40—50°F in the winter. Propagation is by seeds sown in sandy soil in early spring, when the temperature should be 55—60°F. Root cuttings of the perennials can be taken in late winter or early spring and rooted in a cold frame.

Linum (li-num)

From the old Greek name, *linon,* used by Theophrastus (*Linaceae*). Flax. This important genus contains, besides the economically valuable annual which supplies flax and linseed oil, a number of very decorative garden plants. The flower color which is characteristic of the genus is a fine pale blue, but there are a number of shrubs with yellow blossoms and a lovely scarlet annual. The genus is widely distributed in the temperate regions of the world.

1 The yellow flowered Linum 'Gemmell's Hybrid' is a very floriferous plant.
2 Linum narbonense, a favorite garden plant, is a native of Europe.

Species cultivated Perennial: *L. alpinum,* 6 inches, blue, July—August, Alps. *L. campanulatum,* 1 foot, yellow, June—August, south Europe. *L. capitatum,* 9 inches, yellow, June—August; south Europe, Asia Minor. *L. flavum,* 1—1½ feet, yellow, June—August, Germany, Russia. *L. hirsutum,* 15 inches, blue with white eye, summer, south Europe, Asia Minor. *L. monogynum,* 2 feet, white, June—July, New Zealand. *L. narbonense,* 2 feet, blue, May—July, south Europe. *L. perenne,* 1½ feet, blue, June—July, Europe. *L. salsoloides,* 9 inches, pink, June—July, south Europe.

1 *Lobelia cardinalis, the Cardinal Flower, is a 3 foot high perennial.*
2 *The tall Lobelia tupa bears red flowers in autumn.*
3 *The yellow flowered Lupinus arboreus is the short lived Tree Lupin.*
4 *The bicolor Lupin 'Vogue' is a good cultivar.*

Lupinus (lu-py-nus)

From the Latin *lupus,* a wolf (destroyer), because it was thought that the plants depleted the fertility of the soil by sheer numbers (*Leguminosae*). Lupin. A genus of over 300 species of annuals, perennials and subshrubs, mainly from North America, though there are a few Mediterranean species which, since Roman times, have been used for green manuring. This is surprising, since the Roman farmers did not know that within the root nodules were colonies of bacteria capable of utilizing nitrogen to produce valuable nitrates. The fine Russell hybrid lupins are among the most showy of herbaceous perennials and have a wide color range embracing the three primary colors: red, yellow and blue. They do not, however, thrive on alkaline soils.

Perennial species cultivated *L. nootkatensis,* 1 foot, blue, purple and yellow, May — July, northwest America. *L. polyphyllus,* 4 feet, blue, white or pink, June—August, California.

Shrubby: *L. arboreus,* 6 feet, short lived, yellow, white or violet, fragrant, summer, California. *L. excubicus,* 1—5 feet, blue, violet, summer, California; var. *hallii* (syn. *L. paynei*), larger flowers.

Russell hybrids These well loved hybrids have developed from a cross made at the end of the last century between *L. arboreus* and *L. polyphyllus.* Some years later a seedling with rose-pink flowers appeared, *L. p. roseus,* and with the help of this,

George Russell was able to develop and select the superb colors and strong spikes that are available today in the now famous Russell strain.

Some good cultivars are: 'Betty Astell', 3 feet, deep pink; 'Blue Jacket', 3 feet, deep blue and white; 'Fireglow', 3 feet, orange and gold; 'George Russell', 4 feet, pink and cream; 'Gladys Cooper', 4½ feet, smoky blue; 'Joan of York', 4 feet, cerise and pink; 'Josephine', 4 feet, slate blue and yellow; 'Lady Diana Abdy', 3½ feet, blue and white; 'Lady Fayne', 3 feet, coral and rose; 'Lilac Time', 3½ feet, rosy-lilac; 'Mrs Micklethwaite', 3 feet, salmon-pink and gold; 'Mrs Noel Terry', 3 feet, pink and cream; 'Thundercloud', 3 feet, blue and rose-mauve.

Cultivation The most popular are the perennial species, easily grown in any sunny border that has not too much lime. Mulch with compost in spring and cut down the old flower stems in October.

The Russell lupins are now available from seed, though the named forms are still raised from cuttings of young growths in March. These are not among the longest lived plants and it is wise to renew them from time to time. Since they are hardy they may be raised from seed sown

in drills ½ inch deep in April and replanted in the autumn. Many will flower during the following summer.

The tree lupin, *L. arboreus,* may be raised from seed with ease. These shrubs make rapid growth, and will flower in their second season. They are, however, not long lived, but generally manage to renew themselves by self sown seedlings. The shrubby lupin, *L. excubicus,* makes a fine large plant, but needs some frost protection. Like most lupins, this has very fragrant flowers.

Lychnis (lik-nis)

From the Greek *lychnos,* a lamp, alluding to the brilliantly colored flowers (*Caryophyllaceae*). This small genus from the north temperate zone of the Old World contains some good herbaceous perennials and one good hardy annual. Two of our most impressive wild plants, the red and the white campion belong here, and, in fact, are worthy of garden cultivation, the white one in particular for its extreme fragrance in the evening. There is a natural hybrid between these two plants which has delicate pink flowers. The ragged robin, *L. flos-cuculi,* is also a plant

quite worth growing in the garden. It is interesting that *L. chalcedonica* gives us the brightest scarlet in the herbaceous garden, while *L. flos-jovis* (syn. *Agrostemma flos-jovis*, *A. coronaria flos-jovis*) gives us a magenta to accompany its grayish foliage.

Species cultivated *L. alba* (syn. *Melandrium album*), white campion, 3 feet, May to August, Europe. *L alpina* (syn. *Viscaria alpina*), 6 inches, pink, summer, Europe. *L. arkwrightii*, 1½ feet, scarlet, summer, hybrid. *L. chalcedonica*, 3 feet, scarlet, summer, Russia. *L. coeli-rosa* (syn. *Silene coeli-rosa*), rose of heaven, 1 foot, purple and various other colors, annual, Levant; *L. coronaria*, 2½ feet, magenta, July and August, south Europe. *L. dioica* (*Melandrium rubrum*), the red campion, 3 feet, strong pink, summer, Britain. *L. flosculi*, 1½ feet, ragged robin, rose-pink, May and June, Britain. *L. fulgens*, 9 inches, vermilion, May to September, Siberia. *L. grandiflora* (syn. *L. coronata*), 18 inches, salmon, summer, Japan. *L.* × *haageana*, 9 inches, very large scarlet flowers, hybrid. *L. lagascae* (syn. *Petrocoptis lagascae*), 9 inches, rose and white, summer, Pyrenees. *L. viscaria* (syn. *Viscaria vulgaris*), catchfly, 1 foot, reddish-purple, summer, Europe.

Cultivation Most lychnis are very easily grown in any kind of soil and can withstand dry conditions better than many other herbaceous plants. However, *L. alpina* and *L. lagascae* need richer soil. Some of these herbaceous plants are rather short lived perennials—*L. alba* is almost biennial. All may be readily raised from seed sown in March in the open garden, as they are supremely hardy.

Lysimachia (lis-e-mak-e-a)

Probably from either *Lysimachus*, King of Thracia, or from the Greek *luo*, to loose, and *mache*, strife, hence the common name of *L. vulgaris* (*Primulaceae*). This genus, of which most species in cultivation are hardy herbaceous perennials, has some species which have long been cultivated. There are about 120 species in all from temperate and subtropical regions of the world, three of them being British natives.

1 The golden leaves of Lysimachia nummularia aurea, the Creeping Jenny, make a useful and attractive ground cover.
2 Lychnis chalcedonica is a brightly flowered herbaceous perennial.
3 Lychnis dioica, the Red Campion, is a native of Britain.
4 The yellow flowered Lysimachia punctata reaches 3 feet and spreads quickly.
5 Lythrum salicaria, the Purple Loosestrife, has several cultivars such as 'Rose Queen', shown here.

The yellow loosestrife and creeping jenny are cultivated in gardens, the latter plant makes an excellent specimen for a hanging basket with its neat leaves and abundance of yellow flowers.

Species cultivated *L. atropurpurea*, 2 feet, purple, summer, Greece. *L. clethroides*, 3 feet, white, summer, foliage brightly colored in autumn, Japan. *L. ephemerum*, 3 feet, white, summer, Europe. *L. fortunei*, 3 feet, white, summer, China and Japan. *L. leschendultii*, 1 foot, rose-red, summer, India, does best in light, sandy soil. *L. nemorum*, creeping, yellow, summer, Britain. *L. nummularia*, creeping jenny, yellow, summer, Britain; var. *aurea*, golden leaves. *L. punctata* (syn. *L. verticillata*), 3 feet, yellow, summer, Europe. *L.*

thyrsiflora, 3 feet, yellow, summer, north Europe. *L. vulgaris,* yellow loosestrife, 3 feet, yellow, summer, Britain.

Cultivation Rich moist soil is appreciated by these plants, and many many species do best by the sides of pools or streams. They will tolerate some shade. The soil needed in hanging baskets or pots for *L. nummularia* consists of 1 part soil, 1 part organic matter and 1 part sand. The baskets should be suspended in partial shade. This plant also makes a useful ground cover under trees, particularly in its golden leaved form. Propagation is by division of plants in spring or autumn.

Lythrum (lith-rum)

From the greek *lythron,* black blood, in reference to the color of the flowers of some species (*Lythraceae*). Loosestrife. This is a small genus, mainly consisting of hardy herbaceous and shrubby perennials from temperate regions. One of them, *L. salicaria,* makes the banks of many streams beautiful, and it grows abundantly in wet meadows, its long flower spikes coming in late summer when flowering wild plants are beginning to be scarce.

Species cultivated *L. alatum,* 3 feet, crimson-purple, July to October, North America. *L. salicaria,* purple loosestrife, 3 feet, crimson-purple, July, Britain; cultivars include 'Brightness', rose; 'Prichard', rose-pink; 'The Beacon', deep crimson. *L. virgatum,* 2—3 feet, crimson-purple, summer, Taurus; 'Rose Queen', rosy-red, is a less tall cultivar.

Cultivation These are ideal plants for the borders of ponds and streams. However, provided the soil is moist, these loosestrifes will grow in any border. The plants should be lifted and divided periodically, and this is the best method of propagation. It should be done in October or April.

Macleaya (mac-lay-a)

Commemorating Alexander Macleay, 1767-1848, Secretary of the Linnean Society (*Papaveraceae*). This genus, sometimes listed under the synonym *Bocconia,* consists of two Chinese species of perennial herbaceous plants very valuable in the garden. Their most outstanding virtue is their great height (8 feet or more) which lifts their large, airy heads of tiny petalless flowers and unusual rounded and lobed leaves above less statuesque plants. Because of their bold and dignified appearance they are useful specimen plants to stand as isolated eye catchers, although a group of them is even more impressive.

Species cultivated *M. cordata* (syn. *Bocconia cordata*), plume poppy, tree celandine, 8—12 feet high, leaves 8 inches across, white beneath and containing an orange colored sap which oozes out of any cut or broken surface, buff flowers in graceful panicles, summer. *M. microcarpa* (syn. *Bocconia microcarpa*), similar to the

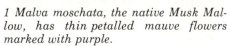

1 *Malva moschata, the native Musk Mallow, has thin petalled mauve flowers marked with purple.*
2 *The blooms of Malva sylvestris, a British native, are foxglove purple.*
3 *Macleaya cordata, the Plume Poppy, reaches 8—12 feet and bears filmy summer flowers of pale coral.*

former, but the flower plumes are somewhat more yellow in color, and the plant is somewhat shorter; 'Kelway's Coral Plume' is a cultivar with coral-pink buds.

Cultivation Rich soils suit these plants, which should also have full sun. They do very well on well drained alkaline soils. They should not require staking, except in very exposed situations, as they have stout hollow stems. Since they sucker rather freely, detachment of suckers in early summer provides the most suitable method of propagation. If a clump is being dug up

for transplanting it is essential to remove every piece of root, otherwise new plants will eventually appear even from quite small pieces of root left in the soil.

Malva (mal-va)

From the Greek *malakos,* soft or soothing, probably in reference to an emollient yielded by the seeds (*Malvaceae*). A genus of hardy herbaceous perennial and annual plants. *M. moschata,* the musk mallow, is one of the most decorative of wild flowers, quite suitable for the herbaceous border. It is even more lovely in its white variety. All

parts of the musk mallow are said to give off a musky odor when taken indoors, especially in warm, dry weather. It is unfortunate that in some areas all malvaceous plants are afflicted by *Puccinia malvacearum,* the hollyhock rust.

Species cultivated *M. alcea,* 4 feet, rosy-purple, summer, hardy perennial, often grown as annual, Europe; var. *fastigiata,* flowers red, July to October. *M. crispa,* 5 feet, purple and white, summer, annual, Europe. *M. moschata,* 3 feet, rose or white, summer, perennial, Europe including Britain; var. *alba,* white. *M. sylvestris,* 3 feet, purple, summer, biennial, Europe including Britain.

Cultivation In general, these plants will grow in any kind of soil and in most aspects, though the annuals need sunny conditions to give their best. All can be easily raised from seeds sown in sandy soil in spring under glass at a temperature of 55°F. The perennials will flower in their second season.

Meconopsis (mek-on-op-sis)
From the Greek *mekon,* a poppy, and *opsis,* like (*Papaveraceae*). This genus of poppy like and very showy annual, biennial and perennial plants generally attracts much attention in those fortunate gardens which

1 *The white flowered Meconopsis superba has a central boss of golden anthers which enhances the bloom.*
2 *Meconopsis regia, a native of Nepal, is attractive summer and winter, as a basal rosette of silvery leaves remains after the plant has finished flowering.*
3 *Meconopsis grandis, with its delicate, deep blue summer flowers, is a native of Sikkim.*

provide the necessary conditions for their cultivation. Most of the showy Chinese and Himalayan species need light woodland conditions and a moist soil or climate. Very many of these plants are monocarpic, that is, they will die after they attain flowering age whether it be in one, two, three or more years' time. It is probably the bright blue species which are most admired, though some of the delicate yellow ones are extremely fine.

One species, *M. cambrica,* the Welsh poppy, is a British native which, with its golden-yellow or orange flowers will brighten sunny or shady places in the garden and will successfully seed itself, often in such inhospitable places as between the cracks in paving stones or even between the bricks in old walls where the pointing has decayed.

Species cultivated (monocarpic unless

otherwise noted) *M. aculeata*, 15 inches—2 feet, pale blue-violet, summer, western Himalaya. *M. betonicifolia* (syn. *M. baileyi*), blue poppy, blue Himalayan poppy, 4 feet, azure blue, June to July, Himalaya. *M. cambrica*, 1½ feet, yellow, summer, Europe including Britain, perennial; vars. *aurantiaca*, flowers orange; *plena*, flowers double, orange or yellow. *M. delavayi*, 6 inches, violet, summer, western China. *M. dhwojii*, 2½ feet, primrose yellow, summer, Nepal. *M. grandis*, 3 feet, blue, June, Sikkim, perennial; 'Branklyn' is a form with large, rich blue flowers. *M. horridula*, 3½ feet, blue, red or white, Asia. *M. integrifolia*, 6 inches, violet, Central Asia. *M. napaulensis*, 5 feet, pale mauve and pink, June, Himalaya. *M. paniculata*, 5 feet, yellow, July to August, Western China. *M. punicea*, 1½ feet, crimson, autumn, Tibet. *M. quintuplinervia*, 1½ feet, lavender-blue, Tibet. *M. sarsonii*, 2—3 feet, sulphur yellow, summer, hybrid. *M. simplicifolia*, 2 feet, purple to sky blue, summer, Himalaya. *M. sinuata*, 2 feet, pale blue, May to June, east Himalaya. *M. superba*, 4 feet, pure white, May and June, Tibet, Bhutan. *M. villosa*, 2 feet, buttercup yellow, July, Himalaya, perennial.

Cultivation A woodland soil containing leaf mold is most suitable, and some light overhead shade during part of the day is appreciated. It is advisable to sow the seeds as soon as they are available in autumn, but if you get your seeds from a commercial source they will not be available until the

1 Mimulus cardinalis, the Cardinal Flower, is a summer flowering perennial with red and yellow flowers.
2 The perennial Mimulus guttatus, Monkey Musk, has yellow flowers splotched with red in summer.

spring. A few species, such as *M. quintuplinervia* may be propagated by division; others, for example *M. grandis*, may be increased by removing and rooting sideshoots. Many of the species, especially those with rosettes of silvery leaves, are suited to the lower stratum of the rock garden. Water generously in summer but keep dry in winter. In general the meconopsis do better in moist conditions. It is a challenge to attempt to grow this perennial.

Mimulus (mim-u-lus)
From the Greek *mimo,* ape; the flowers were thought to look like a mask or monkey's face (*Scrophulariaceae*). Monkey flower, monkey musk, musk. A genus of hardy annual, half hardy perennial and hardy perennial plants, grown for their showy flowers. They are found in many temperate parts of the world, particularly in North America.
Species cultivated Annual *M. brevipes,* to 2 feet, yellow flowers, summer. *M. fremontii,* 6—8 inches, crimson flowers, summer. Hardy perennial *M. × burnetii,* 1 foot, yellow, spotted bronze; var. *duplex* flowers double. *M. cardinalis,* cardinal monkey flower, 1—2 feet, red or red and yellow

flowers, summer. *M. cupreus,* 8—12 inches, flowers yellow to copper-red, summer; cultivars include 'Monarch Strain', 1 foot, various colors; 'Red Emperor', 6 inches, scarlet flowers; 'Whitecroft Scarlet', 4 inches, bright orange-scarlet flowers. *M. guttatus* (syn. *M. langsdorfii*), 1—1½ feet, yellow, red spotted flowers, summer. *M. lewisii,* 1—1½ feet, red or white flowers, late summer. *M. luteus,* 1½ feet, yellow flowers, summer. *M. moschatus,* monkey musk, 9 inches, yellow flowers, summer. *M. primuloides,* 2—3 inches, creeping habit, yellow, June and July. *M. ringens,* 2 feet, violet to white flowers, summer. *M. variegatus,* 1 foot, blotched flowers, summer, best grown as a half hardy annual. Cultivars include 'Bonfire', 9 inches, orange-scarlet flowers; 'Queen's Prize', 9 inches, white, cream and yellow, blotched red flowers.

Cultivation Annual species do best in moist, shady positions, though they will grow in sunny places provided the soil is sufficiently moist. Propagation is by seed sown under glass at a temperature of 55—65°F in spring. The seedlings are pricked off, and gradually hardened, finally in a cold frame, before being planted at the end of May or the beginning of June. The hardy perennials grow well in sun or shade, provided the soil is moist. They should be planted from spring to early summer. Propagation is by seed sown from spring to early summer in a temperature of 55—60°F, by cuttings of young growths inserted in sandy soil at almost any time at a

temperature of 55—65°F, or by division of established plants in spring.

Monarda (mon-ar-da)
Named after a sixteenth century Spanish physician and botanist, Nicholas Monardes (*Labiatae*). A small genus of annual and perennial herbs native to North America, with fragrant leaves and flowers, related to *Salvia*. The leaves are nettle like and the flowers have a spiky appearance and are clustered together in whorls: the color ranges from white through pink, mauve and purple to red.

Species cultivated *M. didyma,* bee balm, oswego tea, 2—3 feet, scarlet flowers, sometimes in twin whorls, late summer; cultivators include 'Adam', 2½ feet, cerise; 'Beauty of Cobham', purple leaves, pink flowers; 'Cambridge Scarlet', crimson-scarlet; 'Croftway Pink', soft pink; 'Dark Ponticum', dark lilac; 'Melissa', soft pink; 'Pale Ponticum', lavender; 'Pillar Box', bright red; 'Sunset', 4 feet, purple-red. *M. fistulosa,* wild bergamot, 4—5 feet, purple flowers, summer, not as showy as *M. didyma;* var. *violacea* (*Violacea superba*), deep violet-purple. *M. menthaefolia,* similar to *M. fistulosa,* with mint like foliage.

Cultivation Any ordinary garden soil will suit these plants but there must be plenty of moisture and good drainage. They will grow in sun or partial shade. They can be planted in the autumn or spring and need top dressing. Propagation is by division in February or March, or they can be raised from seed sown out of doors in a semi-shaded position in spring or in boxes placed in the greenhouse or cold frame in March. Seeds germinate easily, but the plants will need rogueing and any drab colored varieties discarded.

Nepeta (nep-ee-ta)
An early Latin name, probably taken from an Italian place name Nepi (*Labiatae*). A genus of about 150 species of hardy herbaceous perennials and annuals, a few of which are grown partly for their aromatic foliage. Some were once used for their remedial properties. One, grown commonly under the name of *N. mussinii,* often used for edging, is of hybrid origin and is more

1 Nepeta x faassenii is a silvery-lavender summer flowering perennial frequently used as an edging plant in bedding schemes.
2 Oenothera biennis, the very fragrant Evening Primrose, is a native of North America and the West Indies.
3 Oenothera fruticosa 'Yellow River' is a good, free flowering herbaceous perennial for the border.

correctly called *N.* × *faassenii.* Creeping kinds can be usefully grown as ground cover in shady places.

Species cultivated *N.* × *faassenii* (syn. *N. mussinii* of gardens), 1—1½ feet, silvery foliage, flower spikes formed by whorls of soft lavender-blue flowers with darker spots, May to September, hybrid, *N. cataria,* catmint, catnip, 2—3 feet, flowers whitish-purple in whorls on upright stems, summer. *N. macrantha* (syn. *Dracocephalum sibiricum*), 3 feet, blue flowers clustered on stems, summer. *N. nervosa,* 1—2 feet, light blue flowers in dense spikes, July-September. Cultivars include 'Six Hills Giant', 2½ feet, light violet flowers, summer; 'Souvenir d'André Chaudron', 1 foot, rich lavender-blue flowers, July-September.

Cultivation The nepetas will do well in ordinary well drained soil in sunny borders, grouped or as edging plants. As growth is vigorous and sprawling, it is inadvisable to plant nepetas too near smaller plants which may easily be smothered. Plant in autumn or spring. Cutting back

dead autumn growth should be delayed until the spring when the new growth begins. Then the plants should be trimmed to remove the dead stems. Propagation is by seed sown in spring, division in spring or cuttings taken from new growth made from base of plants cut back in summer after flowering. Young shoots root readily in sandy soil in a cold frame and can be planted in the following spring.

Oenothera (ee-noth-er-a)
From the Greek *oinos,* wine, and *thera,* pursuing or imbibing, the roots of one plant being thought to induce a thirst for wine (*Onagraceae*). A genus of 80 species of annuals, biennials and numerous good herbaceous and shrubby perennials for the herbaceous border and rock garden, natives of America and the West Indies, but now widely naturalized in many parts of the world. The flowers, fragrant in many species, are fragile in appearance, carried in racemes or singly in the leaf axils and generally yellow but there are white, pink and red forms. The common name, Evening Primrose, relates to *O. biennis* in particular, the flowers opening in the evening.

Species cultivated *O. acaulis,* trailing, flowers white, aging to rose, spring to autumn, hardy perennial. *O. biennis,* biennial, 3 feet, yellow, very fragrant, June—October. *O. erythrosepala* (syn. *O. lamarckiana*), 4 feet, flowers yellow, aging to reddish, to 3½ inches across, summer to autumn, probably of garden origin. *O. fruticosa,* about 2 feet, lemon yellow flowers, July and August, one of the best of the herbaceous perennials. *O. glaber,* 1½ feet, foliage bronze-green, flowers golden-yellow, summer. *O. missouriensis,* about 9 inches, trailing and spreading in habit, bright, light yellow flowers, July, perennial. *O. odorata,* to 1½ feet, flowers yellow, turning red, to 2½ inches across, opening in the evening, April to June, perennial; var. *sulphurea,* taller, later flowering, leaves, buds and stems tinted red. *O. perennis* (syn. *O. pumila*), 1 foot, flowers yellow, opening in daylight, July, perennial. *O. speciosa,* 2 feet, white flowers, scented at night, appearing throughout the summer and early autumn, perennial, United States, Mexico. *O. tetragona* (syn. *O. youngii*), 2 feet, flowers yellow, to 1½ inches across, opening by day, summer; var. *riparia,* 1½ feet, flowers larger. Cultivars: 'Fireworks', 1½ feet, bright red buds opening to yellow flowers, makes a very good plant for the front of the border; 'Yellow River', 1—1½ feet, canary yellow, very free flowering.

Cultivation These plants are sun lovers; they do well in any ordinary soils, including those that contain much lime. The trailing kinds are suitable for the rock garden, taller kinds for sunny borders. They can be propagated by division in spring or they may be grown from seed. Seed of the biennial species is best sown in May or June where the plants are required to flower, the flowers being produced the following year in July and August. Cuttings of the perennial species can also be taken in May and rooted in a sandy soil.

Paeonia (pe-o-ne-a)

Commemorating *Paeon,* an ancient Greek physician, said to have first used *P. officinalis* medicinally. Although the genus has long been considered a member of the buttercup family, *Ranunculaceae,* some modern botanists now place it in a family of its own, *Paeoniaceae.* A genus of 33 species of hardy herbaceous and shrubby perennials and a few shrubs, among the noblest and most decorative plants for a sunny or shaded border. The main division of the genus is between the herbaceous and the

1 Paeonia mlokosewitschii, a native of the Caucasus, bears single yellow spring flowers held high above the grey-green foliage. 2 Paeonia 'Sarah Bernhardt' is a beautiful fully double hybrid whose pale pink petals are tipped with silver. 3 The hybrid Paeonia x 'Esperance', the result of a cross between Paeonia lutea and Paeonia suffruticosa, has large yellow semi double flowers.

tree peony, but botanically the matter is much more complex. Stern's monograph, *A Study of the Genus Paeonia,* published by the Royal Horticultural Society in 1946, deals with the whole classification. The wild herbaceous species are single flowered and vary in height from about 1 foot up to 3 or 4 feet. The double varieties have been developed by breeding and selection. The tree peonies, although woody shrubs, are deciduous and are often grown in association with other hardy perennial plants. They enjoy a sunny position but are liable to be broken by winds so should be planted in a reasonably sheltered place. Long established specimens — they live many years — may attain a height of 7 feet or more with a considerable spread. Accordingly it is necessary to allow ample space when planting tree peonies for no peony likes being moved once it has been planted. Tree peonies are often grafted on to the rootstock of *P. officinalis,* the common garden peony, and

when planting, care should be taken to bury the point of the union between the stock and the scion 3 inches below the surface. It is at this point that a young specimen may be broken in rough weather. If possible choose a site that does not get the early morning sun because tree peonies come into growth earlier than herbaceous varieties and the young shoots may be damaged by late spring frosts.

Species cultivated *P. anomala,* 1—1½ feet, foliage finely cut, flowers bright crimson, May, Russia, central Asia. *P. bakeri,* 2 feet, flowers purplish-red, May, possibly of garden origin. *P. broteri,* 1—1½ feet,

purplish-red, May, Spain and Portugal. *P. cambessedesii,* 1½ feet, deep rose-pink, April-May, Balearic Isles, liable to damage by spring frost. *P. clusii* (syn. *P. cretica*), 1 foot, white, May, Crete. *P. coriacea,* 1½—2 feet, rose, April, Spain, Morocco. *P. delavayi,* up to 5 feet, shrubby, dark red, May, China; var. *angustiloba,* leaves finely divided. *P. emodi,* 1—3 feet, white, May, Himalaya. *P. humilis,* 15 inches, distinct small leaflets, dark pink to red, May, southern France, Spain. *P. lactiflora* (syns. *P. albiflora, P. edulis*), up to 2 feet, white, fragrant, June, Siberia, northern China, Mongolia. *P. lutea,* shrubby, up to 4½ feet,

yellow, June, China, Tibet. *P.* × *lemoinei* (*P. lutea* × *P. suffruticosa*), shrubby, 4—5 feet, flowers large, yellow, May—June. *P. mascula* (syn. *P. corallina*), 2—3 feet, deep rose, May, Europe. *P. mlokosewitschii,* 1½ feet, foliage, gray-green, flowers yellow, coral stamens, April, Caucasus. *P. officinalis,* up to 2 feet, red, May, southern Europe; vars. *albo-plena,* the old double white peony; *rosea plena,* the old double rose peony; *rubra plena,* the old double crimson peony. *P. peregrina* (syns. *P. decora, P. lobata*), up to 3 feet, deep maroon-red, May, southern Europe, Asia Minor. *P. potaninii* (syn. *P. delavayi angustiloba*),

shrubby, up to 5 feet, deep maroon, May, western China. *P. suffruticosa* (syn. *P. moutan*), tree peony, up to 6 feet, rose-pink, May, China, Tibet. *P. tenuifolia*, 1—2 feet, leaves finely dissected, fern like, flowers deep crimson, May, Transylvania, Caucasus. *P. veitchii*, 1—2 feet, purplish-red, June, China. *P. wittmanniana*, up to 3 feet, yellowish, April, Caucasus.

Hybrid Double Peonies (a selection) 'Adolphe Rousseau', 3 feet, maroon, golden anthers, large, June. 'Alice Harding', 2½ feet, pale pink, cream within, fragrant, excellent foliage on strong stems, May and early June. 'Baroness Schroder', 3 feet, free flowering, white, with yellow center, large globular blooms excellent for cutting, fragrant, late May and June. 'Claire Dubois', 3 feet, satiny pink and silver, June. 'Duchesse de Nemours', 3 feet, free flowering, white to pale sulphur yellow, medium size, incurved bloom, fragrant, May and June. 'Edulis Superba', 3 feet, old rose-pink, edged silver, fragrant, early May onwards, much used as a commercial variety for cut bloom. 'Eugene Verdier', 3 feet, soft pink, silver edged, free flowering, a famous old variety, June. 'Felix Crousse', 2½ feet, bright deep carmine, large, a popular variety. 'Festiva Maxima', 3 feet, pure

1 *Paeonia 'Lady Alexandra' is a good summer flowering rose pink specimen.*
2 *Paeonia 'Bowl of Beauty' is an outstanding cultivar with pink petals and cream petaloid stamens in the center, giving the effect of a fine anemone flowered bloom.*
3 *The single flowered Paeonia 'White Wings' with its bright yellow central boss of stamens holds its flowers well above the foliage.*
4 *Paeonia delavayi is a shrubby type growing up to 5 feet in height with dark crimson summer flowers.*
5 *There are many named forms of the herbaceous Paeonia which appear in a wide range of color.*

white, flecked crimson, fragrant, a splendid old variety, the name meaning the largest and gayest, May. 'Germaine Bigot', 2½ feet, semi double, glistening white, shaded pale salmon, fragrant, June. 'Karl Rosenfeld', 2½ feet, bright crimson, June. 'Kelway's Glorious', 2½ feet, creamy-white, large, fragrant, among the best of the doubles, May—June. 'Sarah Bernhardt', 2½ feet, bright pink, tipped silver, large, June.

Hybrid Single Peonies 'Eva', 2½ feet, deep salmon-pink, June. 'Lady Wolseley', 2½ feet, deep rose, large, June. 'Lord Kitchener', 3 feet, deep maroon-red, May. 'Pink Delight', 2 feet, pale pink, becoming white, May.

Cultivation Peonies are easily grown in sun or partial shade and in deep fertile soil, preferably well limed, where they can re-

1 The pink flowers of Paeonia 'Queen Elizabeth', like most of the single kinds, have prominent golden yellow stamens.

2 The semi double Paeonia 'Asian Jewel' is a deep mauve-pink rather loose in flower form.

3 Paeonia suffruticosa 'Rock's Variety' is a cultivar of Paeonia suffruticosa, the Moutan Paeony, better known as the Tree Paeony. The white bloom with deep purple blotches low on each petal appears in May.

4 Paeonia 'Souvenir de Maxime Cornu', a Paeonia lutea hybrid, has apricot yellow double flowers.

5 The fragrant, summer flowering Paeonia lactiflora is a native of Siberia and Mongolia. It has given rise to a number of garden cultivars known as Chinese Peonies, among the easiest of all perennials to grow.

6 Paeonia lutea is a shrub, growing to 4 or 5 feet, with dark green leaves with a glaucous underside and cup like blooms.

1 Red is the rarest tint in the extensive range of color to be found in the Pansy family.
2 There is a good range of bedding Pansies which bloom from late winter onwards.
3 The colorful display provided by Pansies in the herbaceous border can be prolonged by removing dead flower heads.
4 The attractive markings on the pansy add variety to the numerous strains.

main undisturbed for many years. Top dress with old manure or garden compost in February every two or three years. Named varieties of herbaceous peonies are increased by division in September or October, which gives the newly planted pieces time to make fresh roots before the ground is frozen. Great care must be taken when lifting the clumps for division, as the thick rootstock is very brittle. Peonies can be raised from seed, but it is a slow process and the seedlings may vary considerably in color and form. Seed should be sown about 2 inches deep in sandy loam in a cold frame in September. Newly gathered seed is best. With old seed the covering may be hard and the seed should be soaked in water for a few days before sowing. Some seeds may germinate the first spring, but the majority may take up to two years. Placing seed in a refrigerator for 48 hours or so before sowing sometimes accelerates germination. Seedlings may take five years or more to develop into plants large enough to produce mature blooms. One cannot assess accurately the quality of the blooms from

those produced in the first and second year of flowering as they are not usually typical. Grafting in August is done by commercial growers, usually on stock of *Paeonia albiflora.* Tree peonies can also be layered, but it is a slow process, and air layering has been attempted on a small scale without great success.

Pansy

The pansy and the viola are very similar and belong to the same family (*Violaceae*). Pansies are used mainly for summer bedding, although they can be treated as perennials and increased by means of cuttings. This is, in fact, what is done to perpetuate outstanding varieties for show purposes. In most gardens, however, pansies are treated as biennial plants and discarded after flowering. There are a number of different colorful strains which have been produced by crossing *Viola tricolor* with selected varieties — 'Monarch Strain', 'Engelman's', 'Roggli' of Swiss origin, and 'Morel's' — or by hybridizing different strains. The work continues and there is no telling what splendid flowers will appear in the years to come. What is known as the Fancy Pansy is grown for exhibition purposes and has superseded the Show Pansy. For show work the flower should be large, circular in outline, with smooth, thick, velvety petals without serrations. The middle of the flower should be slightly convex with the petals gently re-

flexed. The colors should be harmonious, with a margin of uniform width, and the yellow eye large, bright and clearly defined. The flower should be not less than 2½ inches in diameter.

Cultivation Pansies thrive in well drained, deeply dug soil that has been enriched with superphosphate and compost. Choose an open position, preferably with some shade from the midday sun. Where the soil is heavy, fork in gritty material—old weathered ashes, sharp sand, — or compost and a dressing of lime may help increase the tilth. With such a soil the bed should be raised about 6 inches above the surrounding level. On light soil dig in manure and garden compost some weeks before planting time.

Planting may be either in the autumn or in the spring, but this depends upon local conditions. Plants put out in the autumn will usually start to flower earlier than those bedded in spring; however, in heavy soil it is wise to defer planting until the spring. Where plants are put out in autumn, top dress the bed or border with equal parts of loam, sedge peat or leaf mold and sharp sand a week or two after planting. This will prove a useful protection to the roots during the winter. The plants are reasonably hardy but will not withstand excessive winter moisture. When planting is done in the spring, this should be during the second half of March, weather permitting. Set out the plants about 10—12 inches apart and during dry weather water them freely in the evenings.

Propagation is by seed sown in light soil in boxes or pans in July or August and placed in a cold, shady frame. Transplant the seedlings into their flowering positions in September or early October, or plant in pots and overwinter in a cold frame. Outstanding plants may be increased by cuttings taken in August or September and inserted in sandy soil in a cold, shady frame, or by division in September or October. For exhibition purposes allow one bloom only to grow on each shoot, removing other buds at an early stage. Plants grown for exhibition should be fed weak liquid fertilizer once a week throughout the growing season (see also Viola).

Strains and cultivars include 'Cardinal Giant', brilliant red. 'Chantreyland', apricot. 'Coronation Gold', yellow flushed orange. 'Early Flowering Giant', sky-blue. 'Engelmann's Giant', mixed colors. 'Felix' strain, large flowers, various colors, yellow centers. 'Feltham Triumph', various colors. 'Indigo Blue', blue with dark blotches. 'King of the Blacks'. 'Masquerade', various light color combinations. 'Pacific Toyland F_2 Hybrids', mixed colors. 'Paper White'. 'Roggli', mixed colors, very large flowers. 'St. Knud', lower petals orange, upper apricot. 'Westland Giants', mixed colors, very large flowers.

Winter flowering kinds (flowering from February onwards). These include 'Celestial Queen', sky blue. 'Helios', golden-yellow. 'Ice King', white with dark spots. 'Jupiter', sky blue with a purple blotch. 'March Beauty', velvety purple. 'Moonlight', primrose yellow. 'Orion', golden-yellow. 'Winter Sun', golden-yellow with dark spots.

Pansy stem rot This is a disease usually referred to as pansy sickness, in which the stem base and roots rot and the plant turns yellow. It is common among pansies and violas and it is necessary to plant in new ground. Do not plant too deeply. The fungus responsible for the stem rot is *Myrothecium roridum*.

Papaver (pap-a-ver)

An ancient Latin plant name of doubtful origin, but possibly derived from the sound made in chewing the seed (*Papaveraceae*). Poppy. A widespread genus of 100 species of colorful hardy annual and perennial plants. Poppies like full sun, although some will flower reasonably well in partial shade. The newly unfolded petals have the appearance of crumpled satin and many varieties have a glistening sheen on the blooms. They produce seed freely and many hybrids have been raised which are very decorative and easily grown. When used as cut flowers they will last longer if the stems are burned when they are cut before putting them in water. This seals the milky sap in the stems.

Perennial species cultivated *P. alpinum,* 6 inches, bluish-green foliage in neat tufts, yellow, orange, salmon and white flowers, summer, Europe. *P. atlanticum,* 18 inches, orange flowers, summer, Morocco. *P. nudicaule,* Iceland poppy, yellow, white and orange flowers, summer, subarctic regions. *P. orientale,* Oriental poppy, 3 feet, orange-scarlet, June, Asia Minor. *P. pilosum,* 2 feet, leaves form a green hairy rosette, orange-buff flowers, summer, Asia Minor. *P. rupifragum,* Spanish poppy, 2 feet, soft terra-cotta pink flowers, summer, Spain.

Papaver orientale, the Oriental Poppy, a native of Asia Minor, usually has a dark blotch at the base of each petal. The petals themselves are inclined to flop.

Cultivars There are many delightful varieties of the poppies in many and diverse colors; the following is a selection from those currently available. The annual varieties include the Shirley poppies, derived from *P. rhoeas,* single, and one of the best of all annuals; the double 'Ryburgh' hybrids and the begonia flowered, also double in many colors and both also derived from *P. rhoeas;* from *P. somniferum* come the 'Daneborg' hybrids, scarlet with fringed petals and four white inner petals, the carnation flowered also fringed, the peony flowered doubles, and 'Pink Beauty', 2½ feet, with gray leaves and double salmon-pink flowers. The perennial varieties include those from *P. nudicaule,* such as 'Coonara', salmon pink and rose; 'Golden Monarch', 'Kelmscott Strain', rich mixed colors; 'Red Cardinal', crimson-scarlet; 'Tangerine', brilliant large orange flowers. Also varieties of *P. orientale* such as 'Beauty of Livermere', scarlet frilled flowers; 'Grossfurst', crimson; 'Lord Lambourne', orange-scarlet; 'Princess Victoria Louise', cerise-pink; 'Olympia', light orange-scarlet, double early; 'Queen Alexandra', rose; 'Perry's White', white with dark blotches; 'Rembrandt', orange-scarlet; 'Salmon Glow', salmon-pink, double; 'Watermelon', single large, cherry-red.

Cultivation Sow annual varieties in April in patches where they are to flower. They prefer a sunny position and reasonably good soil. Thin the seedlings to 2 or 3 inches apart when quite small. Plant the perennial varieties in October or early spring in deeply dug, loamy soil in full sun, and top-dress with compost in March or April. Propagation of the perennials is by means

1 Papaver orientale has numerous forms.
2 Papaver 'Mrs. Perry' is one of the best known and popularly grown of the cultivars of Papaver orientale.

of root cuttings in winter, by division of the roots in March or April or by seed sown in pans or boxes in a cold frame in spring or on a finely prepared seed bed out of doors in early summer, scarcely covering the fine seeds. *P. alpinum* and *P. nudicaule* are frequently grown as annuals or biennials (for the Welsh poppy see Meconopsis).

Pelargonium (pel-ar-go-knee-um)

From the Greek *pelargos,* a stork, referring to the resemblance between the beak of the fruit and that of a stork (*Geraniaceae*). This is the correct name for the plant which is grown in public parks and our gardens and greenhouses. The zonal pelargoniums have in the past 70 years mostly been called 'Geraniums' which is a complete misnomer. The true Geraniums were described earlier.

Within the past 10 years the horticultural public has been made aware of the misnomer, mainly by the efforts of the specialist societies throughout the world, and are now using the correct term for the zonal and regal pelargoniums in increasing numbers.

To help to sort out the confusion that has existed, it is worth stating that the cultivars of the genus *Pelargonium,* both regal and zonal types, have definitely been bred from the true *Pelargonium* species and not from the genus *Geranium;* this is the key to the correct definition.

In the genus *Pelargonium* there are over 300 recorded species; this does not include the sub species and other varieties not yet recorded, of which there must be a considerable number.

The species are identified in one way by the fact that the plants breed true from seed, although some have individual races within the species which also breed true from seed, and a lot of cross-pollination is done by insects on plants growing in their natural habitat, causing much confusion among taxonomists. Many of these natural hybrids are very closely identified with the original plant but may have slightly different leaves, form or flowers.

The species were mainly brought to Europe from many parts of Africa, although several places in other parts of the world such as Australia, New Zealand and Tasmania have also contributed during the last three centuries. They are not hardy in cooler zones and have to be protected during the winter months, although a wide range of species is grown out of doors in some places.

What is remarkable is that such a large number of colorful cultivated varieties could ever have been bred from plants that have only very small flowers. It shows the tenacity and enthusiasm of the breeders who performed this task, mainly during the last century, although this work is still underway.

The species are fascinating to explore, and there is no doubt that they are more important than the cultivars in many ways, especially in their use for hybridizing purposes and also for experimentation and research.

There are many kinds of fantastic shapes and forms among the various kinds and a great number have scented fragrance in their leaves. Although this scent is often clearly defined, it cannot be assessed absolutely in all varieties because so many factors contribute to the amount of volatile oil in the tissues. Variations can be caused by environment, feeding, soil structure, age of plants, time or season of year, etc., all of which can vary by region. Another reason smells or perfumes seem to vary is because the sense of smell varies widely among different persons. The volatile oil is distilled from many of the species for use in cosmetics and perfumes.

The scented leaved kinds are listed here because they are mainly species and thus they are easy to classify.

The leaves of some pelargoniums are edible and are used in cooking and can add at least ten different flavors to any cake. It is, therefore, worthwhile growing certain species for this purpose alone.

The following is a list of the species most commonly known and grown. If they do have a perfume this is described in terms which are generally accepted for the particular species. Except where stated all species are natives of South Africa, and, in general, they all flower in summer and normally grow to between 9 inches and 2½—3 feet in height.

Species cultivated *P. abrotanifolium,* flowers white or rose veined with purple, leaves fragrant of southernwood (*Artemisia abrotanum*). *P. acetosum,* leaves silvery-green, tasting of sorrel, single carmine flowers, can be used in cooking. *P. angulosum,* plant hairy, leaves 5 lobed, flowers purple, veined maroon. *P. australe,* flowers rose or whitish, spotted and striped carmine, Australia, New Zealand, Tasmania. *P. capitatum,* rose scent, pale mauve blooms. *P. crispum,* strong lemon scent, flowers pink or rose; vars. *major,* large; *minor,* smaller; *variegatum,* lemon scent, gray-green leaves with cream edges, very elegant for floral display work. *P. cucullatum,* rose scented cupped leaves, flowers red with darker veins, late summer, a parent of the regal pelargoniums and very good for outdoor pot plant growing. *P. denticulatum,* sticky leaves with strong undefined scent, flowers lilac or rosy-purple, best species with fern like foliage. *P. echinatum,* sweetheart geranium, tuberous rooted, stems spiny, leaves heart shaped, lobed, flowers purple, pink or white. *P. filicifolium* (syn. *P. denticulatum filicifolium*), fern like leaves, very pungent scent, small rose flowers. *P. formosum,* salmon flowers, white tipped, upright habit. *P. × fragrans,* nutmeg scented geranium, small dark green leaves

1 *Pelargonium* 'Carisbrooke' has soft rose-pink petals with darker markings.
2 *The white flowers of Pelargonium* 'Muriel Harris' *are feathered with red.*
3 *Pelargonium* 'Black Prince'.

smelling of spice, flowers white, veined red; var. *variegata*, a miniature plant with a very pleasant scent, tiny light green leaves edged with cream, easily grown and propagated, should be in every collection. *P. frutetorum*, prostrate habit, salmon flowers. *P. gibbosum*, gouty pelargonium, so named because the joints are similar to those on elderly people so afflicted, flowers greenish-yellow, early summer. *P. graveolens*, rose scented geranium, strong rose scent, flowers pink, upper petal with dark purple spot; used in the distillation of perfume. *P. inquinans*, scarlet flowers, plain leaves, one parent of the zonal pelargoniums. *P. multibracteatum*, leaves heart shaped, deeply lobed, with dark green zones, flowers white. *P. odoratissimum*, apple scented geranium, leaves heart shaped or kidney shaped, fragrance of apples, flowers small, white. *P. peltatum*, ivy leaved geranium, leaves fleshy, flowers pale rosy-mauve, a parent of the ivy leaved cultivars. *P. quercifolium*, oak leaved geranium, leaves roughly oak leaf shape, grey-green, strongly scented, flowers mauve. *P. radula*, fern like leaves, fragrant of verbena, flowers rose, upper petals blotched purplish-carmine, very attractive if grown out of doors during the

1 The flowers of Pelargonium 'Mrs. Lawrence' are rose pink.
2 The double white flowers of Pelargonium 'Gonzale' make a compact head.
3 Pelargonium 'Salmon Irene' bears full heads of coral-pink blooms.
4 Pelargonium 'Harvester' produces a consistently rounded head.

summer when it grows into a small shrub. *P. saxifragioides*, very dainty plant with tiny leaves similar to some ivy leaved kinds, flowers mauve, marked purple. *P. tetragonum*, often called the cactus type pelargonium because of its four sided stems; its growth should be controlled by topping because of its vigorous habit, flowers small, white, single. *P. tomentosum*, strong peppermint scent, leaves gray-green, soft and spongy, sometimes difficult to keep during the winter period, flowers tiny, white. *P. tricolor*, foliage sage green, small tricolor flowers, lower petals white, upper petals magenta, with dark spots, a good plant for pots in the greenhouse, a prize collector's piece. *P. triste*, the sad geranium, tuberous rooted, long, much divided leaves, flowers brownish-yellow with a pale border; sweetly scented in the evening. *P. zonale*, flowers single, mauve,

pink or red, leaves lightly zoned. 'Lady Plymouth', foliage as *P. graveolens* except that the leaves are variegated green and lemon. 'Mabel Grey', strong lemon scent, upright grower that needs frequent topping. 'Prince of Orange', orange scented, small pale mauve flowers.

The 'Uniques' are another group that have sprung up in recent years and are stated to be *P. fulgidum* hybrids. *P. fulgidum*, a subshrubby species with bright red flowers, is prominent in their ancestry. They are best grown in pots and hanging baskets. There are many different perfumes in the leaves of the varieties listed below:

'Crimson Unique', red and black flowers; 'Scarlet Unique', lemon scent, red flowers, parent of 'Carefree' and 'Hula'; 'Paton's Unique', verbena scent, rose flowers; 'Purple Unique', peppermint scent, purple flowers; 'Rose Unique', rose scent, rose flowers; 'White Unique', white flowers with purple veins. Cultivars: one of the most important sections of the cultivars are the regal or domesticum Pelargoniums which have beautiful flowers and green leaves, but recently some sports have been discovered with golden and green bicolor leaves which should make these beautiful

from 'Grand Slam', 'Lavender Grand Slam'.

A great advantage in growing plants in this section is that they are rarely troubled by disease. The worst pest is the greenhouse white fly which appears at all times and can spread rapidly. It can, however, be controlled by using a good insecticide.

The section which dominates the genus consists of the hortorums, usually referred to as zonals. These are divided into many groups which are classified as follows (selected cultivars are listed under each heading):

Single flowered group (normally will not have more than five petals):

'Barbara Hope', pink; 'Block', scarlet; 'Countess of Jersey', salmon; 'Doris Moore', cherry; 'Elizabeth Angus', rose; 'Eric Lee', magenta; 'Francis James', bicolor flowers; 'Golden Lion', orange; 'Highland Queen', pink; 'Maxim Kovaleski', orange; 'Mrs E. G. Hill', pink; 'Pandora', scarlet; 'Pride of the West', cerise; 'Victorious', scarlet; 'Victory', red. Semi doubles:

American Irenes of various shades and colors are extremely useful for bedding purposes; many named cultivars are very similar to each other. Other cultivated varieties include 'Dagata', pink; 'Genetrix', pink; 'Gustav Emich', scarlet; 'King of Denmark', pink; 'Pink Bouquet', pink; 'The Speaker', red.

Double-flowered group:

'Alpine Orange', orange; 'A. M. Maine', magenta; 'Blue Spring', red-purple; 'Double Henry Jacoby', crimson; 'Jewel', rose; 'Jean Oberle', pink; 'Lerchenmuller', cerise; 'Monsieur Emil David', purple; 'Maid of Perth', salmon; 'Mrs. Lawrence', pink; 'Paul Reboux', red; 'Rubin' red; 'Schwarzwalderin', rose; 'Trautleib', pink.

Cactus group (single or double flowers with quilled petals):

'Attraction', salmon; 'Fire Dragon', red; 'Mrs. Salter Bevis', pink; 'Noel', white; **1** 'Spitfire', red with silver leaves; 'Tangerine', vermilion.

2 Rosebud group (flower buds tight and compact, center petals remaining unopened, like small rosebuds):

'Apple Blossom Rosebud', pink; 'Red Rambler', red; 'Rosebud Supreme', red.

Miniature group:

'Alde', pink; 'Caligula', red; 'Cupid', pink; 'Goblin', red; 'Jenifer', carmine; 'Grace Wells', mauve; 'Mephistopheles', red; 'Mandy', cerise; 'Pauline', rose; 'Piccaninny', red; 'Taurus', red; 'Timothy Clifford', salmon; 'Wendy', salmon; 'Waveney', red.

Dwarf group:

'Blakesdorf', red; 'Emma Hossler', pink; 'Fantasia', white; 'Miranda', carmine;

plants much sought after if hybridizers are successful in breeding these colored leaves into this group.

The main parents of the regals are *P. cucullatum* and *P. betulinum* which are indigenous to the coastal regions of South Africa. Hybridization started on the species mainly in England and France and in central Europe well over a century ago. These plants should be grown under glass or in the house throughout the year in cool areas, although they may be grown out of doors in summer in exceptionally protected places.

Some recommended cultivars are as follows (dominating colors only are mentioned): 'Annie Hawkins', pink; 'Applause', pink and white; 'Aztec', strawberry pink and white; 'Blythwood', purple and mauve; 'Caprice', pink; 'Carisbrooke', rose pink; 'Doris Frith', white; 'Grand Slam', red; 'Marie Rober', lavender; 'Muriel Hawkins', pink; 'Rapture', apricot; 'Rhodamine', purple and mauve; and the outstanding sport

1 The decorative uses of the Pelargonium are numerous if the plants are protected from frost, such as on this conservatory wall.

2 Pelargonium quercifolium is described by its common name, the Oak leaved Geranium.

'Madam Everaarts', pink; 'Pixie', salmon. Fancy leaved group (the colors given are those of the flowers):

Silver leaves: 'Flower of Spring', red; 'Mrs Mappin', red; 'Mrs. Parker', pink; 'Wilhelm Langguth' (syn. 'Caroline Schmidt'), red.

Golden leaves: 'Golden Crest'; 'Golden Orfe'; 'Verona'.

Butterfly leaves: 'A Happy Thought'; Crystal Palace Gem'; 'Madame Butterfly'.

Bronze bicolor leaves: 'Bronze Corrine'; 'Bronze Queen'; 'Gaiety Girl'; 'Dollar Princess'; 'Maréchal MacMahon'; 'Mrs. Quilter'.

Multicolored leaves: 'Dolly Varden'; 'Lass o' Gowrie'; 'Miss Burdett-Coutts', 'Henry Cox'; 'Mrs. Pollock'; 'Sophie Dumaresque'.

Ivy leaved group:

One of the best in this group is *P. peltatum,* the original species from which this section has been derived. Cultivars are: 'Abel Carrière', magenta; 'Beatrice Cottington', purple; 'Galilee', pink; 'La France', mauve;

1 Take cuttings of Pelargoniums in mid to late summer from the tops of the lateral shoots about 3 inches in length. Remove the bottom leaves with a sharp knife.

2 Trim the cutting back to a node.

3 Using a dibble, insert the cutting in a 3 inch pot filled with a sterile rooting compost.

4 The cuttings need to be kept moist to encourage rooting, and as they progress, they can be repotted.

'L'Elegante', leaves cream and green with purple markings; 'Madame Margot', white and green leaf; and two with green leaves and white veins, 'Crocodile' and 'White Mesh'.

In general the large flowered cultivars described above will grow under normal garden and greenhouse conditions as will the colored leaved cultivars, which benefit from being grown outside during the summer months to get full sunshine and rain.

The miniature and dwarf types are best grown in the greenhouse in pots, or they are very useful plants to grow out of doors in containers such as window boxes or urns. They are especially good for hanging baskets when used in conjunction with ivy leaved kinds.

Hanging baskets are very useful for enhancing a display out of doors, especially on porches. One of the best cultivars for this purpose is 'The Prostrate Boar', a newer introduction which grows very quickly and produces an abundance of flowers throughout the summer. Make sure that you get the prostrate type and not the ordinary 'Boar' which does not grow so vigorously, nor flower so freely. 'The Boar', or *P. salmonia,* is inclined to grow vertically.

P. frutetorum has had in the past, and should have in the future, a great influence on the pelargonium genus because of its great vigor and its ability to influence the

pigments in the leaves of the many cultivars crossed with it.

Hybridization merely consists in taking the pollen from one flower and transferring it to the stigma of another compatible cultivar. This method will give some good results, but if you are planning a proper breeding program you should isolate those plants intended for breeding purposes and keep records of each individual cross. This is very necessary if any of your seedlings happen to be good ones and you wish to register them as new introductions. The miniatures and the dwarfs are very adaptable for crossbreeding, so it is advisable to work on these for primary experiments.

Cultivation In general, pelargoniums grown in pots will do well in most good potting mixtures, though it is advisable to add a little extra lime to neutralize the acidity of the peat. Alternatively, particularly for potting rooted cuttings, a suitable soil mixture consists of 2 parts good loam, 1 part sand, 1 part peat, all parts by bulk, and 1 cupful of ground limestone per bushel of the mixture (if the loam is acid). The ingredients should be thoroughly mixed together and then watered with a liquid fertilizer with a high potash content. Some growers have been successful with the 'no

1 The dwarf Pelargoniums are well suited to rock gardens.
2 The Ivy leaved Pelargonium with its distinctively shaped, fleshy foliage grows particularly well in hanging baskets out of doors.

soil' composts (peat/sand mixtures plus balanced fertilizers), while others use ordinary good garden soil which has been sterilized to kill harmful soil organisms.

Pelargoniums should never be over potted. When repotting becomes necessary it is often possible, by removing old compost and slightly reducing the size of the root ball, to replant in the same pot; otherwise the plants should be moved into pots one size larger. They should always be potted firmly.

Although plants should be watered freely during the growing period in spring and summer, they should never be over watered and, in any case, the pots in which they are grown should have openings for drainage and the soil mixture should be free draining so that surplus moisture can get away quickly, otherwise various root rots and stem rots may be encouraged. In winter, plants will need little water, though the soil in the pots should not be al-

lowed to dry out completely.

Some shading will be required in the greenhouse from late April or early May onwards. A light application of whitewash or other proprietary shading compound to the glass will be sufficient.

In order to prevent damping off of the flowers the atmosphere in the greenhouse should be kept as dry as possible during the summer. This means that proper use should be made of the ventilators and that every attempt should be made to keep the air circulating to avoid an over humid, stagnant atmosphere. During the winter, when it is equally important to keep the air dry but warm, good circulation can be provided by using an electrical blower heater.

To keep the plants growing freely and to maintain good leaf color it is necessary to feed them during the growing season. Regular weak applications of proprietary liquid fertilizer should be given from about a month after the plants are in their final pots, until September. It should be noted, however, that plants in the fancy leaved group should either not be fertilized at all, or the fertilizer they are given should not contain nitrogen. These kinds should, in any case, be given less water than others.

A number of zonal varieties can be induced to flower in winter, when blooms are always welcome. The method is to take cuttings in the spring, by normal propagation methods described below. The young plants are grown in pots during the summer. Plants treated in this way should flower throughout the winter months. It is best to maintain a minimum temperature of 60°F and the plants should be given as much light as possible. During the summer the plants may be placed in a sunny cold frame or the pots may be plunged in a sunny, sheltered place out of doors. They should be brought into the greenhouse in September.

Plants which are to be used for summer bedding purposes are raised from cuttings taken in the fall and winter months, rooting several in each 5 inch pot, or in boxes, spacing the cuttings 2 inches apart. In February the rooted cuttings are potted in individual 3 inch pots and kept in a temperature of 45—50°F until April. They are then hardened in a cold frame before planting them out of doors in May or when all danger of frost is over. Do not plant shallowly; it is best to dig a hole large enough and deep enough to take the plant up to its first pair of leaves. Leggy plants may be planted more deeply. Remove dead leaves and flowers as soon as they are seen and pinch out long, unwanted shoots to keep the plants bushy. Keep the plants well watered in dry weather. In September, or before the first frosts, the plants are lifted and brought into the greenhouse for the winter. The shoots should be cut back, long roots trimmed and the plants potted in small pots. The minimum winter temperature in the greenhouse should be around 42°F.

Propagation of regal pelargoniums is by cuttings, which, like those of the other types, root easily. They should be about 3 inches long, taken from the top of the lateral shoots. They are trimmed back to a node and the bottom leaves are removed. They will root quickly in a sterile soil mixture, in pots or in a propagating frame in the greenhouse. Bottom heat is not required. Cuttings of this type are usually taken in late summer.

Propagation of the hortorums or zonal pelargoniums may be done in several ways. Cuttings of the type described above may be taken and either rooted singly in 2½ inch pots or three cuttings may be inserted around the edge of a 3 inch pot. If large numbers are to be rooted they may be inserted in a light soil mixture in a frame, or 2 inches apart in shallow boxes. Cuttings are usually taken in the fall before frost. They may be rooted in a propagating case in the greenhouse, and commercially they are rooted in quantity by mist propagation methods, using bottom heat.

The leaf axil (or leaf bud) method of taking cuttings has become popular in recent years. This consists of taking a leaf and ½ inch of stem from the parent plant, ¼ inch above and below the node or joint. The stem section is cut vertically through the center

of the stem. The cuttings thus formed are inserted in the propagating mixture in the normal way, just covering the buds. If some bud growth is seen in the leaf axils you are more certain of rooting the cuttings. Such cuttings are normally taken in the summer months.

Whichever method you adopt, make sure that you use clean stock only. Almost any piece of a zonal pelargonium containing stem and leaves can be used for propagation purposes, provided the conditions are right. It is quite easy to root stem cuttings of these plants out of doors during the summer months, in the open ground.

Plants may also be raised from seed obtained from a reliable source. It is unwise to buy unnamed seedlings as they may produce large plants with few flowers. Seeds should be sown $1/16$ inch deep in light sandy soil, in pans or boxes, in the greenhouse, from January to April, at 55—65°F.

The leaf axil method of propagating Pelargoniums is a popular way.
1 Cut the stem ¼ inch above and below the node.
2 Also cut the stem vertically through the center.
3 Set the cutting in a pot of clean, damp rooting compost.
4 When inserting the cutting into the compost, allow it to just cover the bud.
5 Pelargonium 'Dolly Varden' is an attractive decorative variety.

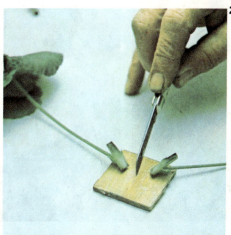

Tuberous rooted pelargonium species may be divided in spring.

The principal pests of pelargoniums grown under glass are aphids and greenhouse white fly. These may be controlled by insecticidal sprays or by fumigation. The disease variously known as black leg, black rot, black stem rot or pelargonium stem rot, is very liable to attack cuttings and sometimes mature plants. It first appears on the lower part of the stem, which turns black. It spreads rapidly up the stem and soon kills the plant. It seems to be encouraged by too much moisture in the soil and by very high humidity. Some control may be obtained by spraying or dusting plants with captain in the autumn. It is also important not to damage the surface of the stem when taking cuttings, otherwise disease spores may enter through the skin at this point. Always use a sharp, clean knife or razor blade when taking or trimming cuttings.

Gray mold (*Botrytis cinerea*) will attack plants under glass, especially in close, humid conditions. It appears as a gray furry mold on stems, leaves or flowers. Proprietary fungicides based on copper or thiram will control this disease, but it is more important to maintain the correct conditions in the greenhouse, with ample ventilation and a moderate humidity. When plants are over wintered, remove all dead or yellowing leaves. When taking away discolored leaves do this by removing the leaf only at first, leaving the stalk intact until the abscission layer has formed

1 The dark leaves contrast with the deep red flowers of Pelargonium 'Red Black Vesuvius'.
2 Pelargonium 'Decorator' has magenta blooms and attractive bicolor leaves.
3 Pelargoniums can be trained as standards by removing all lateral shoots.

between stalk and stem, when the stalk may be removed easily. To attempt to remove it before the abscission layer has formed will result in the stem being damaged with the consequent risk of disease spores entering.

Penstemon (pen-ste-mon)

From the Greek *pente*, five, and *stemon*, stamen, referring to the five stamens (*Scrophulariaceae*). This genus of over 250 species of hardy and half hardy herbaceous annuals, perennials and subshrubs is almost exclusively North American. The name is sometimes erroneously spelt *Pentstemon*. The very popular late summer bedding penstemons were derived from a cross of *P. cobaea* and *P. hartwegii,* and they have a fairly wide color range through pinks and reds to deep maroons and purples. *P. heterophyllus* is a fine subshrub with blue flowers which usually attracts interest when well grown. Another striking plant is the herbaceous *P. barbatus* (syn. *Chelone barbata*), a tall grower, to 3 feet, with bright vermilion-scarlet flowers.
Species cultivated *P. angustifolius,* 1 foot, soft blue, July, western United States. *P. antirrhinoides,* 3 feet, lemon-yellow, July, California. *P. azureus,* 1 foot, blue, August, North America. *P. barbatus,* 3 feet, scarlet, summer, Colorado. *P. barrettiae,* 1 foot, bright violet, May—June, western United States. *P. bridgesii,* 2 feet, scarlet, July to September, North America. *P. campanulatus,* 2 feet, rosy-purple, violet

1 *Penstemon hirsutus (syn. P. pubescens latifolius) is a summer flowering North American native.*
2 *The unusual blooms of Penstemon 'George Home' appear in summer.*
3 *Penstemon rupicola is a native plant of northwestern U.S.*

Mountains. *P. hartwegii*, 2 feet, scarlet, summer, Mexico. *P. heterophyllus*, 1—3 feet, sky blue, July, California. *P. hirsutus* (syn. *P. pubescens latifolius*), purple or violet, 1—3 feet, July, United States. *P. isophyllus*, subshrubby, 4—5 feet, crimson-scarlet, white within, late summer, Mexico. *P. laevigatus*, 3 feet, white or pink, summer, United States. *P. menziesii*, 6 inches, purple, June, northwestern America. *P. ovatus*, 2 feet, blue to purple, August to October, United States. *P. richardsonii*, 2 feet, violet, summer, United States. *P. rupicola*, 4 inches, ruby, northwestern America. *P. scouleri*, 1½ feet, purple, May to June, United States. *P. spectabilis*, 4 feet, rosy-purple, summer, Mexico and southern California.

Cultivars

The following are some good cultivars: 'Blue Gem', azure-blue, summer; 'Chester Scarlet', summer; 'Evelyn', pink, May—October; 'Garnet', wine red; 'George Home', summer; 'Newberry Gem', pillar box red; 'Six Hills Hybrid', rosy-lilac, May—June.

Cultivation A rich, slightly acid soil is most suitable or a mixture of 1 part of leafmold or peat and 2 parts of good loam. A sunny location is required. A weekly watering with a soluble fertilizer or liquid manure is needed by the summer bedding

penstemons to keep them growing and flowering well. Seed is available for many species. This should be sown under glass in February or March at a temperature of 55-65°F and the young plants are set out in May after they have been hardened off. But to get exactly similar plants of hybrids it is necessary to take cuttings and raise them under glass in August. They should not be disturbed until the following April. Plants may also be divided in April.

Phlox (flocks)

From the Greek *phlego,* to burn, or *phlox,* a flame, referring to the bright colors of the flowers (*Polemoniaceae*). A genus of nearly 70 species of hardy, half hardy, annual and perennial herbaceous plants all, with one exception, natives of North America. Almost all the most important species are from the eastern United States, though the popular annual, *P. drummondii,* is from Texas and New Mexico. The fine herbaceous plants derived originally from *P. paniculata,* the garden forms of which may sometimes be listed as *P. × decussata,* play an important part in the garden as they give color during July and August. They are extremely easy to grow and all have fragrant flowers. Our rock gardens would be much poorer if they lacked the various forms of either *P. douglassi* or *P. subulata* or their hybrids.

Herbaceous perennial species cultivated *P. carolina,* 2 feet, phlox-purple to pink and white, May and June, eastern United States. *P. glaberrima,* 2 feet, red, May and June, eastern North America in

or white, June, Mexico and Guatemala. *P. centranthifolius,* 3 feet, scarlet, summer, California and western Arizona. *P. cobaea,* 2 feet, purple or white, August, United States. *P. confertus,* 1 foot, purple and blue, summer, Rocky Mountains. *P. cordifolius,* 4 feet, scarlet, summer, partial climber, southern California. *P. davidsonii,* 1—2 inches, ruby-red, summer, spreads by underground stems, rock garden. California. *P. diffusus,* 2 feet, blue or purple, September, western North America. *P. fruticosus,* 9—12 inches, purple, summer, northwestern United States; var. *crassifolius,* with minor leaf differences. *P. glaber,* 2 feet, purple, July, United States. *P. glaucus,* 15 inches, purple, July, Rocky swamps. *P. maculata,* wild sweet William, 3 feet, violet and purple, summer, eastern North America. These three species are the parents of the early flowering taller phlox. *P. paniculata* (syn. *P. × decussata*), 1½—4 feet, violet purple, summer, eastern North America.

Alpine species cultivated *P. amoena,* 6—9 inches, rose, May to June, southeastern United States; var. *variegata,* leaves variegated with white. *P. bifida,* sand phlox, prostrate, tufted habit, spiny leaves, flowers pale violet to white, spring, eastern North America. *P. divaricata* (syn. *P. canadensis*), 6—15 inches, blue-lavender, May, eastern North America. *P. douglasii* 4 inches, lilac, May to August, western North America. *P. × frondosa,* pink, spring, hybrid. *P. kelyseyi,* 6 inches, flowers lilac, spring, eastern North America. *P. ovata,* 1 foot, rose, summer, eastern North America. *P. pilosa,* 10—20 inches, purplish-rose, summer, eastern North America. *P. × procumbens,* 6 inches, lilac-blue, June, a hybrid. *P. stellaria,* 6 inches, pale blue, April to May, hybrid. *P. stolonifera* (syn. *P. reptans*), 6—12 inches, stoloniferous habit, flowers violet to lavender, 1 inch across, April to May, eastern North America. *P. subulata,* moss phlox, 6 inches, purple or white, eastern United States.

Border cultivars *P. paniculata* is the border perennial phlox which has given rise to many good plants, flowering from July to October, sweet smelling, and very colorful. 'Antoine Mercie', deep mauve with white center; 'Border Gem', deep violet; 'Brigadier', orange-red; 'Europe', white with red center; 'Frau Antonin Buchner', white; 'Jules Sandeau', pure pink; 'Le Mahdi', rich purple; 'Leo Schlageter', dark red; 'Lofna', rose-pink; 'Mrs. A. Jeans', silvery-pink; 'Rijnstroon', rose-pink; 'Starfine', red; 'Thor', salmon-red. Many more will be found in nurserymen's lists.

Alpine cultivars *P. douglasii,* 'Boothman's Variety', clear mauve; 'Eva', pink with deeper centers; 'May Snow', white; 'Rose Queen', silvery pink; 'Snow Queen', white; 'Supreme', lavender-blue. *P. kelseyi,* 'Rosette', stemless pink flowers. *P. stolonifera* 'Blue Ridge', soft blue. *P. subulata* 'Appleblossom', pink; 'Benita', lavender-blue; 'Brilliant', bright rose; 'Camla', clear pink; 'Fairy', mauve; 'G. F. Wilson', mid blue; 'Model', rose; 'Pink Chintz', pink; 'Sensation', rose-red; 'Temiscaming', magenta-red; 'The Bride', white.

Cultivation The tall herbaceous phloxes need a moist loam, preferably on the heavy side. They do perfectly well on limestone soils, provided these are fertilized. They grow best in partial to full sun. Plant from October to March, and fertilize annually with compost and inorganic fertilizers, as they are heavy feeders. Lift, divide and replant every three years. They are readily raised from root cuttings and this has the advantage of providing plants free from the stem eelworm, by which the herbaceous phlox are often attacked.

Alpine phlox species also like a rich soil, and a sunny ledge on the rock garden or on top of a wall. Many of them may be easily increased by layering, or they may be divided (preferably in March). A few of the more dwarf or less vigorous kinds may be given alpine house treatment.

Nematode attack on phlox, by the eelworm species *Ditylenchus dipsaci,* causes bloated and wrinkled foliage, stunted, swollen and split stems and whiptail shoots. The same strain of eelworm will attack gypsophila, oenothera, gladiolus, potato, aubrieta, as well as a number of weeds such as shepherd's purse. Hot water treatment of the dormant stools for one hour at a temperature of 110°F controls the pest. The plants must be returned to uncontaminated soil and infected areas should be kept free of susceptible plants and weeds for at least three years. It is possible to propagate infested phlox without transmitting eelworm by means of seed or by true root cuttings.

1 *Phlox 'Brigadier' is a magenta cultivar of Phlox paniculata.*
2 *Phlox maculata, the Wild Sweet William, is a fine summer flowering herbaceous perennial.*

Physalis (fy-sal-is)

From the Greek *physa*, a bladder, referring to the inflated calyx (*Solanaceae*). A genus of 100 or more species of which the two most well-known are *P. alkekengi*, the Bladder Cherry or Chinese Lantern Plant, with its brilliant, flame colored, air filled calyces, and *P. peruviana*, the Cape Gooseberry, which is a greenhouse species. They are annual and perennial herbaceous plants, mostly from Mexico and North America.

Species cultivated *P. alkekengi* (syns. *P. alkekengi franchetii*, *P. bunyardii*, *P. franchetii*), bladder cherry, Chinese lantern plant, hardy perennial, 1—2 feet, flowers whitish, similar to those of the potato, summer, fruit a single scarlet berry enclosed in the much inflated showy calyx, up to 2 inches long, turning orange in autumn, southeastern Europe to Japan, naturalized in many other parts of the world; vars. *gigantea*, calyces larger; *pygmaea*, 9 inches, dwarf form. *P. ixocarpa*, tomatillo, half hardy annual, 2 feet, flowers yellow, ¾ inch or more across, with black-brown blotches in the throat, fruit purple, sticky, almost filling the yellow, purple veined calyx. The fruits are edible and may be stewed or used for jam making, Mexico, southern United States. *P. peruviana* (syns. *P. edulis*. *P. peruviana edulis*), Cape gooseberry, 3 feet, flowers yellow, blotched purple, summer, fruit yellow, edible, South America, greenhouse. *P. pruinosa*, dwarf Cape gooseberry, strawberry tomato, half hardy annual, 2 feet, flowers bell shaped yellowish, fruits yellow, edible, southern United States.

Cultivation The hardy species require a rich, well drained soil in a sunny or partially shaded position and should be planted in the spring. The fruits, popularly called 'lanterns' (the inflated calyces) can be used for winter decorations and can be picked and dried in autumn. If left out of doors, they become skeletonized. The tender species require a mixture of loam, leaf mold and a little sand and should be planted singly in 5—6 inch pots placed in a sunny position. Water freely during the summer and feed regularly with a liquid fertilizer. Propagate hardy species by division every three years, and greenhouse species from seed sown in sandy soil in the spring or from cuttings placed in sandy soil between January and April. *P. alkekengi* grows very vigorously and spreads by means of underground runners. It may be used as a deciduous ground cover plant in sun or semi shade. Where it is suited it can become something of a nuisance, difficult to eradicate unless every piece of root is removed.

1 Physalis alkekengi, the Chinese Lantern, has papery, air filled calyces of bright orange-red.
2 Pulmonaria angustifolia, the Blue Cowslip, lacks the identifying leaf spots found in other species of the genus.

Pulmonaria (pul-mon-air-ee-a)

From the Latin *pulmo*, lung; derivation uncertain; either because the spotted leaves bore a resemblance to diseased lungs, or because one species was regarded as providing a remedy for diseased lungs (*Boraginaceae*). Lungwort. This is a genus of 10 species of hardy herbaceous perennials, natives of Europe. *P. angustifolia*, is an excellent garden plant. The charm of these early flowering lungworts is in their flowers, which change from red to blue — they also have the name soldiers and sailors on this account — and in their hairy leaves which, in some species, are spotted with a much paler green or with white. The spotted leaves suggested to some herbalists the human lung, and it was thus in accordance with the 'doctrine of signatures' that the plant was used to dose unfortunate sufferers from lung complaints.

Species cultivated *P. angustifolia*, blue cowslip, to 1 foot, leaves lacking spots, flowers pink, changing to blue, spring, Europe including Britain; vars. *alba*, white; 'Mawson's Variety' is a selected garden form. *P. officinalis*, Jerusalem cowslip, spotted dog, to 1 foot, leaves spot-

ted white, flowers pink then violet, spring, Europe. *P. rubra,* 1 foot, leaves usually lacking spots, flowers brick red, Transylvania. *P. saccharata,* to 1 foot, leaves blotched white, flowers pink, April to July, Europe.

Cultivation Any soil is suitable and the plants will grow in sun or shade. The best companions for lungworts are other early spring flowering plants including bulbs, primroses and so on, interspersed with ferns. Plant in autumn or spring and lift and divide the plants every four to five years. Propagation is by seed sown in a shady border out of doors in March or April or by division of the roots in spring or autumn.

Pulsatilla (pulse-a-til-a)

The name was first used by Pierandrea Mattioli, a sixteenth century Italian botanist and physician, and possibly means 'shaking in the wind' (*Ranunculaceae*). This genus of 30 species, distinguished from *Anemone* only by minor botanical differences, includes some of the most beautiful of low growing flowering plants, and one in particular, *P. vernalis,* which is so lovely that it must have converted many to the growing of alpine plants. The plants are very suitable for alpine house cultivation. One of their attractions is the feathery foliage, and another is the equally hairy and feathery seed heads. They are natives of the temperate regions of Europe and Asia.

Species cultivated *P. alpina,* 1 foot, blue buds opening white, May to June, European Alps; var. *sulphurea* with pale yellow flowers. *P. halleri,* 10 inches, flowers of deep violet, finely cut leaves, April to May, Swiss Alps and the Austrian Tyrol. *P. slavica* (syn. *P. vulgaris slavica*), 6 inches, flowers plum-purple with golden centers, April. *P. vernalis,* 6—9 inches, evergreen, finely cut foliage, hairy bronze-violet buds opening to a glistening crystalline white with a mass of golden stamens, April, high Alpine meadows. *P. vulgaris,* Pasque flower, 1 foot, rich purple flowers covered with shaggy fur, April, Europe; vars. *alba,* white; 'Budapest', large powder blue flowers; red flowered seedlings are offered by some nurserymen.

Cultivation A light open soil is suitable; *P. vulgaris* is found naturally on limestone formations. A well drained rock garden suits most species, but they *must* be protected from excess moisture during the winter. It is for this reason that they are so eminently suitable for the alpine house. Seed, sown as soon as it is ripe in July or August, in sandy soil in a cold frame, is the best method of propagation.

1 A red form of Pulsatilla vulgaris has more pronounced color on the inside of the petals.
2 The outstanding purplish flowers of Pulsatilla vulgaris, the Pasque Flower, have bright orange centers.

Pyrethrum (py-re-thrum)

From the Greek *pyr,* fire, probably with reference to fever, since the plant was used medicinally to assuage fever (*Compositae*). These hardy plants are admirable for a sunny border and last well as cut flowers. Long known as pyrethrum they are now botanically classified as *Chrysanthemum.*

Species cultivated *Chrysanthemum coccineum* (syn. *P. roseum*) 1—2 feet, with large, daisy like flowers in May and June. The color is variable from red to white, occasionally tipped with yellow. The leaves are vivid green, graceful and feathery, Caucasus and Persia. There are many hybrids, both single and double. *Single* 2—2½ feet, 'Allurement', rich pink; 'Avalanche', pure white; 'Brenda', bright carmine; 'Bressingham Red', large crimson; 'Eileen May Robinson', clear pink; 'Kelway's Glorious', glowing scarlet; 'Salmon Beauty', bright salmon-rose. *Double* 2—2½ feet, 'Carl Vogt', pure white; 'Lord Rosebery', velvety red; 'Madeleine', lilac-pink; 'Yvonne Cayeux', pale sulphur yellow. For the plant sometimes listed as *Pyrethrum parthenium,* the feverfew, see *Chrysanthemum parthenium.*

Cultivation A well drained loamy soil and a sunny position suit pyrethrums best, though they will grow well on limestone soils. They require ample moisture when coming into bud and during the growing

1 Pyrethrum 'Eileen May Robinson', a clear pink, mixes well with the deep rose of Pyrethrum 'Kelway's Glorious'.
2 The purplish-red flowers of Pyrethrum 'Marjorie Robinson' are single with very prominent central discs.
3 Pyrethrum 'Radiant' is one of many hybrids of Pyrethrum roseum.

season. Plant in March and leave them undisturbed for three or four years. If left longer the plants will deteriorate and the flowers become smaller and fewer. Lift and divide in March or after flowering in July, discarding the old, woody pieces. Each year cut the old flower stems back after flowering. This often results in a second crop of blooms in late summer or autumn. Slugs and rabbits can be a menace but if weathered ashes are scattered around and over the crowns in the autumn this will deter them, as will slug pellets. The plants are somewhat floppy in habit so some light staking should be provided. Propagation is by division in March or after flowering in July, or by seed sown in a cool greenhouse or frame in spring. (See also Chrysanthemum, *C. coccineum*).

Romneya (rom-nee-a)

Named in honor of the Rev. T. T. Romney Robinson (1792-1882), an Irish astronomer who discovered *Romneya coulteri* (*Papaveraceae*). A genus of two species of handsome, semi shrubby perennials from southwestern California with extremely attractive poppy like flowers, borne singly at the ends of the stems.

Species cultivated *R. coulteri,* Californian tree poppy, 6—8 feet, leaves and stems glaucous, flowers satiny white, fragrant, 4—5 inches across, petals frilled, with a prominent mass of golden stamens, throughout the summer. *R. trichocalyx* (syn. *R. coulteri trichocalyx*), similar, but with more erect growth and somewhat larger flowers with a dense covering of bristle like hairs on the calyx. Hybrids are sometimes offered under the name *R. × hybrida* (syn. *R. vandedenii*).

Cultivation These beautiful plants should be planted in April or May in a deep, well drained soil and a sheltered sunny position, preferably beneath a south facing wall where they can spread. Once planted, the roots should be left undisturbed unless the underground stems or roots are required for propagation. They are not suitable for exposed garden spots. Propagation is by root cuttings taken in March or April, about 2 inches long and inserted singly in small pots containing sandy soil and placed in a propagating frame with gentle bottom heat, or seed may be sown in pans of sandy soil in February or March at a temperature of 55°F. Whichever method of propagation is used, the plants should be grown for a year or more in pots before they are planted out in their permanent positions.

Rudbeckia (rud-beck-ee-a)

Commemorating Olaf Rudbeck (1660-1740) Swedish professor of botany and counsellor of Linnaeus (*Compositae*). Cone flower. A genus of about 25 herbaceous plants, mostly perennial and hardy, natives of North America, related to *Echinacea*. The flowers are showy, daisy like, often with drooping petals and conspicuous conical centers. Most of them are excellent herbaceous border plants and are valuable for late summer effect in the garden.

Species cultivated *R. bicolor,* 1—2 feet, half hardy annual, yellow, ray petals yellow, sometimes with purplish bases, disk purplish, conical, July; var. *superba,* flowers 2 inches across, petals brown on the undersides; cultivars include 'Golden Flame', golden-yellow; 'Kelvedon Star', 3 feet, golden-yellow with mahogany red zone; 'My Joy' ('Mon Plaisir'), dwarf habit, flowers golden-yellow. *R. fulgida deamii* (syn. *R. deamii*), 2—3 feet, a somewhat hairy plant of erect habit; flowers deep yellow, 2—3 inches across with purple-black centers, freely produced, July to September; var. *speciosa* (syns. *R. speciosa, R. newmanii*), 2½ feet, similar but of laxer

1 *Romneya coulteri, the California Tree Poppy, is a semi shrubby perennial from the southwestern United States.*
2 *The blooms of Romneya coulteri are satiny white, fragrant and large, measuring from 4 to 6 inches across.*

The daisy like Rudbeckia are distinguished by prominent dark conical centers and showy, often droopy, petals.
1 Rudbeckia 'Bambi' has a red zone at the base of each petal.
2 Rudbeckia 'Herbstsonne' is a tall and very erect hybrid form with down turned petals.
3 Rudbeckia 'Goldsturm' bears large thin petalled flowers in late summer.

habit, an old favorite; 'Goldsturm', 2 feet, an excellent larger flowered form of stiffer habit and less hairy, August—September, a good garden plant. 'Goldquelle', 2½—3 feet, a newer hybrid of erect growth with lemon yellow flowers three or more inches across, August—September. 'Herbstsonne' (*R. laciniata* × *R. nitida*), 6—8 feet, a tall, erect growing plant with large, deeply cut leaves and golden-yellow flowers with green cones, September. *R. hirta*, black-eyed Susan, 2 feet, usually grown from seed as an annual or biennial, a bristly hairy plant, striking flowers in shades of golden, orange and mahogany, summer. *R. laciniata* 'Golden Glow', 6 feet, deeply lobed green leaves and fully double yellow flowers, 3 inches across, August to September. *R. maxima,* 4—6 feet, a rather rare and very ornamental species with large handsome glaucous leaves and rich yellow flowers with dark centers, August—September, Texas. *R. purpurea* see *Echinacea purpurea, R. tetra* 'Gloriosa', Gloriosa daisy, 2—3 feet, half hardy annual, flowers to 7 inches across, colors various including yellow, mahogany-red, bronze, and bicolors; double flowered forms are also offered.

Cultivation Most rudbeckias are easy to grow. A sunny or semi shaded site with good but well drained loamy soil is preferable, though the plants grow well in limestone soils. Some of the taller species and their varieties prefer moister soils and are particularly useful when grown in groups among shrubs or in the wild garden where they provide an early autumn display. Hybrids or cultivars have now largely replaced many of the species in general cultivation. The perennial sorts do best if they are divided and replanted every third or fourth year. *R. hirta* is best treated as an annual and succeeds in a sunny position in well drained soil. Seeds of the half hardy annual kinds should be sown inside in early spring. After they have been hardened the seedlings may be planted out 9 inches apart in late May or early June, where they are to flower. *R. maxima* is rather slow to become established and requires a moist soil. Propagation of the perennials is by seed or by division in the spring.

Salvia (sal-vee-a)

From the Latin *salveo,* meaning save or heal, used by Pliny with reference to the medicinal qualities of some species (*Labiatae*). A large genus of over 700 species of hardy, half hardy and tender annual, biennial, perennial plants and shrubs, some with aromatic leaves, widely distributed in the temperate and warmer zones. It includes the common sage, *S. officinalis,* a valuable culinary plant, as well as many colorful summer and autumn flowering border plants.

Species cultivated *S. ambigens,* about 5 feet, perennial or subshrub, flowers deep sky blue, September—October, South America, slightly tender. *S. argentea,* 2 feet, most decorative, leaves large, silvery-gray, felted, flowers white, small, in spikes, June and July, Mediterranean region; for a dry soil and a sunny position. *S. aurea,* shrub, leaves rounded, covered with fine hairs, flowers yellowish-brown, South Africa, hardy in mild areas. *S. azurea,* 4 feet, subshrub, flowers deep blue, autumn, North America, hardy; var.

grandiflora, flower spikes denser. *S. fulgens,* Mexican red sage, 2—3 feet, shrub, flowers scarlet, in whorls, July, Mexico, tender. *S. gesneraeflora,* 2 feet, sub-shrub, flowers bright scarlet, summer, Colombia, tender. *S. grahamii,* shrub, to 4 feet, flowers deep crimson, July onwards, Mexico, somewhat tender. *S. greggii,* shrub, 3 feet, flowers scarlet, summer, Texas, Mexico, tender. *S. haematodes,* biennial, 3 feet, leaves large, wrinkled, heart shaped, light blue flowers on branching stems from June to August, Greece. *S. interrupta,* 2—3 feet, subshrub, leaves 3 lobed, aromatic, flowers violet purple with white throat, May to July, Morocco, nearly hardy. *S. involucrata,* subshrub, 2—4 feet, flowers rose, summer and autumn, Mexico, not quite hardy; var. *bethelii,* flowers rosy crimson in longer spikes. *S. juriscii,* perennial, 1 foot, flowers violet, June, Serbia, hardy. *S. lavandulifolia,* perennial, 9—12 inches, leaves gray, flowers lavender, early summer, hardy. *S. mexicana minor,* subshrub, to 12 feet in nature, flowers violet-blue, February, Mexico, tender. *S. neurepia,* subshrub, 6—7 feet, flowers scarlet, late summer and autumn, Mexico, hardy in the milder areas. *S. officinalis,* common sage, subshrub, 2—3 feet, leaves wrinkled, aromatic, flowers variable purple, blue or white, June and July, southern Europe, hardy; vars. *purpurascens,* reddish-purple stems and leaves, strongly flavored; *aurea,* leaves golden, flowers rarely produced. *S. pratense,* perennial, 2 feet, flowers bright blue, June to August, Europe, including Britain, hardy; var. *rosea,* flowers rosy-purple. *S. rutilans,* pineapple scented sage, subshrub, 2—3 feet, flowers magenta-crimson, summer, tender. *S. sclarea,* clary, biennial or short-lived perennial, leaves and stems sticky, flowers pale mauve, bracts white and rose, conspicuous, June to September, Europe; various strains are offered; var. *turkestanica,* flowers white, bracts and stems pink. *S. splendens,* scarlet sage, subshrub, 3 feet, flowers scarlet, in spikes in summer, Brazil, usually grown as half hardy annual; vars. for summer bedding: 'Blaze of Fire', 9—12 inches, scarlet; 'Fireball', 15 inches, rich scarlet; 'Harbinger', 15 inches, long scarlet spikes; 'Salmon Pygmy', 6 inches. *S. × superba* (syn. *S. nemorosa*), 3 feet, bracts reddish, persistent, flowers violet-purple in spikes, July to September, hybrid, hardy; var. *lubeca,* identical but 1½ feet tall only. *S. uliginosa,* bog sage, 4—5 feet, leaves shiny green, deeply toothed, flowers azure blue in spikes, August to October, eastern North America, hardy.

Cultivation Salvias are easily grown in ordinary, well drained garden soil and in a sunny position. *S. argentea* particularly likes dry soil, as well as sun, and *S. officinalis* should be cut back in spring to encourage new bushy growth. *S. × superba* makes a particularly good border plant when planted in a bold group. *S. uliginosa* prefers moister conditions than the others,

and its creeping rootstock should be given a winter mulch in cold areas. Those described as tender will succeed in the milder regions, given the shelter of a warm wall, or they may be grown in the greenhouse in pots in a mixture of loam and well rotted manure or leaf mold plus some sand to provide drainage. The pots may be placed out of doors in June and brought in again in September. Water freely from spring to autumn, moderately in winter. Maintain a temperature in winter of 45-55°F. Propagate the shrubs, subshrubs and hardy perennial kinds by division in the spring or by soft wood cuttings, rooted in sandy soil

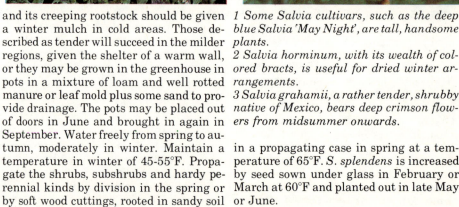

1 Some Salvia cultivars, such as the deep blue Salvia 'May Night', are tall, handsome plants.

2 Salvia horminum, with its wealth of colored bracts, is useful for dried winter arrangements.

3 Salvia grahamii, a rather tender, shrubby native of Mexico, bears deep crimson flowers from midsummer onwards.

in a propagating case in spring at a temperature of 65°F. *S. splendens* is increased by seed sown under glass in February or March at 60°F and planted out in late May or June.

Saxifraga (sax-ee-fra-ga)

From the Latin *saxum,* rock or stone, and *frango,* to break, alluding either to its ancient medicinal use for 'breaking' stones in the bladder or to the supposed ability of the roots to penetrate and assist the breakdown of rocks (*Saxifragaceae*). Saxifrage, rockfoil. A genus of some 370 species of mainly dwarf tufted perennial and annual plants inhabiting the mountain regions of the northern and southern temperate regions. The many species, varieties and cultivars are usually grown in the rock garden or in the alpine house.

For the convenience of classification, the genus is divided into 15 or 16 sections, largely on the basis of the characteristics of its foliage and habit. From the gardener's point of view, however, it is best divided as below into fewer larger groupings according to cultivational requirements.

Species cultivated *S. aizoides,* yellow mountain saxifrage, a loosely tufted mat-forming species with yellow, orange or red flowers and linear fleshy leaves. *S. aizoon* (see *S. paniculata*). *S. apiculata* (*S. marginata × S. sancta*), a cushion or Kabschia hybrid, forming wide mats of green, silver tipped rosettes and primrose yellow flowers on 3 inch stems. *S. × arcovalleyi* (*S. burseriana × S. lilacina*), a Kabschia hybrid with compact silvery cushions and soft pink flowers on 1 inch stems. *S. aretioides* produces hard, gray-green cushions and yellow flowers; a Kabschia that has been the source of many good hybrids easier to grow. *S. × assimilis* (probably *S. burseriana × S. tombeanensis*) has firm gray cushions and white flowers on 1—2 inch long stems. *S. biternata* is similar to *S. granulata* from the Mediterranean area. It has tufts of hoary, kidney shaped, divided leaves and large glistening white flowers on 6—8 inch long stems. *S. × borisii* (*S. ferdinandicoburgii × S. marginata*) is a Kabschia hybrid with blue-gray cushions and large citron yellow flowers on 3 inch stems. *S. boryi,* allied to *S. marginata,* but more compact in habit. *S. × burnatii* (*S. paniculata × S. cochlearis*) is a silver or encrusted hybrid showing a blend of the parental characteristics; white flowers in loose panicles are borne on reddish stems. *S. burseriana* is the finest of the Kabschias and a parent of many excellent hybrids and cultivars. The type plant forms large cushions of crowded, silver gray rosettes composed of many narrow, somewhat spiny, leaves. Each rosette bears a 2 inch long reddish stem surmounted by one or more large glistening white flowers in early spring. *S. b.* 'His Majesty' is a splendid form with the flowers flushed pink; *S. b.* 'Gloria' has larger flowers on redder stems; *S. b. sulphurea* may be a hybrid, but looks like the type plant with soft yellow flowers. *S. cespitosa* (syn. *S. caespitosa*), tufted saxifrage, is one of the 'mossy' species. It makes dense cushions of somewhat glandular, hairy, deeply divided leaves and bears small white flowers on short slender stems. *S.*

caucasica is a green leaved Kabschia with yellow flowers on 1 inch high stems. *S. cernua* may be likened to a mountain form of the meadow saxifrage (*S. grandulata*) with a drooping inflorescence bearing both white flowers and red bulbils in the leaf axils. *S. cochlearis* is an encrusted species, with small spoon shaped silver leaves forming the hummock like plants, from which arise slender panicles of milk white flowers on reddish glandular stems. *S. c. minor* and *major* are smaller and larger forms. *S. cortusifolia* belongs to the Diptera section, to which the better known *S. fortunei* belongs, and has rounded, deeply cut leathery leaves on stiff 3 inch long stems and panicles of white flowers with irregularly sized narrow petals. *S. cotyledon* is one of the largest encrusted species, with broad rosettes of wide strap shaped leaves rimmed with silver and huge airy panicles of white flowers that may be 1½ feet or more long. *S. c. caterhamensis* and 'Southside Seedling' are superior forms with red spotted flowers. *S. crustata,* also an encrusted sort, is smaller, the rosettes forming cushions or mats with off white flowers on branched 6 inch stems. *S. cuneata* is a loose 'mossy' species with toothed, deeply lobed, leathery leaves and open panicles of white flowers. *S. cuneifolia* belongs to the Robertsonia section whose chief representative in gardens is *S. umbrosa*. It is a small species with flat

rosettes of leathery daisy like leaves and flowering stems. *S. cuscucitiformis* is a smaller edition of mother of thousands (*S. stolonifera*) with the leaves prettily veined white. Abundantly produced red stolons, or runners, resemble the leafless stems of common dodder (*Cuscuta*). *S. cymbalaria* is an annual, with smooth shining kidney shaped leaves and numerous starry yellow flowers. *S. decipiens* (see *S. rosacea*). *S. × engleri* (*S. crustata × S. hostii*) resembles the first parent, and has pink flowers on 3 inch stems. *S. exarata* is a distinctive 'mossy' saxifrage, with dark green, strongly nerved, deeply cleft leaves, and flowers that may be either white, yellow or purplish. *S. ferdinandi-coburgii* belongs to the encrusted group, forming neat mounds of silver-gray, spiny leaved rosettes topped by 4 inch high stems bearing red buds and bright yellow flowers. *S. × florariensis* (*S. hostii × S. lingulata*) is an encrusted hybrid eventually forming mats of handsome 3 inch wide, silvered rosettes that turn red in autumn, and have foot long sprays of white flowers. *S. fortunei* is undoubtedly

1 Saxifraga aizoides, the Yellow Mountain Saxifrage, forms loose golden mats.
2 Saxifraga fortunei has panicles of white flowers and kidney shaped leaves.
3 Saxifraga apiculata is a mat forming dwarf type.

the finest member of the Diptera section, with large, glossy, thick textured, kidney shaped leaves which are often red beneath, and tall airy, elegant panicles of glistening white flowers, each with one or more extra long tail like petals. The plant is completely deciduous after the first severe frost of late autumn. *S. × fredericiaugusti* (probably *S. media × S. porophylla*) is a hybrid in the Engleria section, noteworthy for the flowering stems being clad in leafy, often colored bracts. This hybrid has silver rimmed rosettes and flowers composed of a bell shaped calyx covered with claret hairs below the small pink petals. *S. geum* (see *S. hirsuta*). *S. × godseffiana* (*S. burseriana × S. sancta*) produces mats of narrow spiny leaved rosettes and lemon yellow flowers on reddish stems. *S. granulata*, the meadow saxifrage of Britain and also known as fair maids of France, is a deciduous species, the kidney shaped, rounded toothed leaves dying away soon after the plant has flowered; milk white flowers are borne on branched stems up to 1 foot tall; var. *plena* has double flowers. *S. grisebachii* belongs to the Engleria section, eventually forming humped mats of 3 inch wide gray rosettes set with leafy flowering spikes 9 inches tall. The bell shaped calyces and bracts are set with deep red glandular hairs. *S. × haagii* (*S. ferdinandii-coburgii × S. sancta*) is a Kabschia with dark green rosettes in cushions and bears rich yellow flowers. *S. hederacea* rather resembles a small creeping *Linaria* or *Cymbalaria*, with small ivy shaped leaves and starry white flowers. *S. hirculus* is placed in a section of the same name, and forms tufted mats of narrow leaves and branched stems set with quite large yellow flowers speckled with orange. It is a rare British native and known as yellow marsh saxifrage. *S. hirsuta*, probably better known as *S. geum*, is a Robertsonia saxifrage akin to London pride, but with longer leaf stalks and rounded leaves heart shaped at the base, set with long hairs on both surfaces. The flower stems, covered with short hairs, support open panicles of small white blossoms, each petal bearing a yellow spot at its base. *S. hostii* is one of the finest encrusted species, forming wide mats of silvery rimmed rosettes set with creamy white flowers in short corymbs. *S. huetiana* is a small bushy annual with starry yellow flowers freely produced. *S. hypnoides*, Dovedale moss, is a cushion or mat forming mossy species native to most of the hilly regions of the northern temperate zone. It is very variable in habit, flower size and color, the type being white; var. *condensata* is very compact with yellow flowers; var. *kingii* is close growing, the leaves turning red in winter; var. *purpurea* has reddish flowers. *S. × irvingii* (probably *S. burseriana × S. lilacina*) is one of the free blooming Kabschia hybrids with lilac-pink flowers. *S. × jenkinsae* is similar to the preceding and probably of the same par-

1 *Saxifraga x haagii*, a Kabschia Saxifrage, bears golden-yellow blooms.
2 *Saxifraga hypnoides*, the Dovedale Moss, looks most effective in winter when the flowers have died back.

entage. *S. juniperifolia* has dark green, spine tipped leaves rosettes in humped cushions, usually only sparingly set with small yellow flowers. *S. lilacina* produces wide dense mats of small green rosettes set with amethyst flowers on 1 to 2 inch tall stems. This distinctive Kabschia has entered into the parentage of many fine hybrids. *S. lingulata* should now be known as *S. callosa*. It is a very garden worthy encrusted species with mats of large iron-gray rosettes and 1—1½ feet long, gracefully arching panicles of pure white flowers; var. *catalaunica* has shorter broader leaves and shorter, stiffer flowering stems. *S. longifolia* is perhaps the finest of the large encrusted species with huge, densely leafy rosettes and elegant flowering stems up to 2 feet, long branched right to the base. *S. marginata* is another Kabschia that has contributed to some good hybrids; it forms mats or loose cushions of small green rosettes rimmed with silver and bearing short branched stems set with large white flowers. *S. media* is another Engleria somewhat smaller than *S. grisebachii* and which has been a parent of many hybrids. *S. moschata* covers most

of the common 'mossy' hybrids seen in gardens; it is similar to *S. decipiens* in appearance, but usually a little more dwarf and in various shades of red and pink, but sometimes yellow. *S. m.* 'Cloth of Gold', has golden-green foliage and white flowers; 'Mrs. Piper' is a good bright red; 'Elf' is pink; 'James Bremner' is white; and var. *sanguinea superba* is scarlet. *S. oppositifolia* is the familiar purple saxifrage of the mountains of the northern temperate zone, extending down to sea level in the more northern latitudes. This is a variable species as regards flower color and leaf size, though always mat forming with leafy interlacing stems and solitary terminal almost stemless purple flowers; var. *splendens* has large red-purple flowers; 'R. M. Prichard' is lilac-purple; *alba* is a form with white flowers, and *rudolphiana* is bright rose-purple. *S. paniculata* is still usually grown under the name of *S. aizoon*, a very variable encrusted species of great charm; var. *baldensis* (*minutifolia*) is very dwarf and compact growing with small silvery rimmed rosettes in low mounds and 4 inch stems of pure white flowers; var. *lutea* is similar to the type with mounds of stoloniferous rosettes and soft yellow flowers; var. *rosea* has clear pink flowers and reddish leaves; var. *orientalis* has green rosettes and milk white flowers on 4 inch stems. *S. porophylla* is akin to *S. media* and others of the Engleria group, but with purple calyces and small pink petals. *S. retusa* is akin to *S. oppositifolia* but with smaller foliage and the rose-purple flowers in short terminal clusters. *S. rosacea* is still better known as *S. decipiens* and is the main 'mossy' species in cultivation, often as one parent with *S. granulata*, *S. moschata* and others. Most of the cultivars form loose cushions or are mat forming with divided leaves and a profusion of short stemmed flowers in all shades of pink, red and white. Some of the cultivars listed under *moschata* may well belong here. *S. rotundifolia* belongs to the Miscopetalum section which is close to Robertsonia and London pride. It has rounded or kidney shaped leaves in tufts and airy panicles of small starry flowers, white speckled pink; var. *heucherifolia* is smaller, hairier and with flowers more heavily spotted. *S. sancta* forms wide carpets of small rosettes of dark green spine tipped leaves and bears rich yellow flowers on 2 inch tall stems. It is one of the most frequently grown green leaved Kabschias. *S. scardica* is a blue-gray Kabschia, forming hard mounds topped by 4 inch stems of large white flowers sometimes flushed pink. *S. spathularis*, St. Patrick's cabbage, is an Irish native belonging to the Robertsonia section. It resembles a smaller edition of London pride with airy panicles of starry white flowers spotted with yellow and crimson. Crossed with *S. umbrosa* it gives the familiar London pride which thrives in shady town gardens. *S. stolonifera* (syn. *S. sarmentosa*), mother of thousands, or strawberry geranium has long red, branched runners like those of a strawberry, large round marbled rather fleshy leaves and graceful panicles of white flowers spotted with yellow and red. Typical of the Diptera section, each flower has one or two extra elongated petals. *S. trifurcata* belongs among the 'mossy' species with deeply cut recurved leaves somewhat aromatic when bruised and 6 inch stems of large white flowers. *S. umbrosa* is akin to *S. spathularis* but with shorter, long hairy leaf stalks and the leaf blades with a cartilaginous border. *S. valdensis* is similar to, but smaller and slower growing than *S. cochlearis*, with stiff glandular stems surmounted by heads of round white flowers. Cultivars: 'Amitie' (*S. lilacina* × *S. scardica obtusa*) is a Kabschia with firm cushions of gray-green rosettes and lilac flowers on 1 inch stems. 'Apple Blossom' ('mossy' hybrid) has small pale pink flowers in profusion. 'Boston Spa' (Kabschia hybrid) bears deep yellow flowers with red buds over green cushions. 'Buttercup' (Kabschia) has rich yellow flowers on gray-green cushions. 'Cecil Davies' (*S. lingulata* × *S. longifolia*) has very compact mounds of silvered rosettes and elegant sprays of white flowers. 'Cranbourne' is probably the finest of the Kabschia hybrids with neat gray-green mounds of ½ inch wide rosettes and almost stemless large clear pink flowers. 'Dr. Ramsay' (*S. cochlearis* × *S. longifolia*) is an encrusted cultivar with symmetrical silvered rosettes and sprays of white flowers on 1 foot stems. 'Edie Campbell' and 'Elf' are both 'mosses', the former with large pink flowers in profusion, the latter smaller and neater. 'Ester' (*S. paniculata lutes* × *S. cochlearis*) bears soft yellow flowers in short sprays over vigorous masses of silvered rosettes. 'Faldonside' (*S. aretioides* × *S. marginata*) is a first rate Kabschia with citron yellow flowers, the overlapping petals of which are charmingly crimped at the margins. 'Gem' (*S. burseriana* 'Gloria' × *S. irvingii*) is another good Kabschia with neat blue-gray spiny mounds and pale pink flowers with a ruby eye. 'Four Winds' is a rich red 'mossy' sport. 'Iris Pritchard' (*S.* × *godroniana* × *S. lilacina*) bears flowers of apricot-rose over neat gray hummocks 'James Bremner' is one of the few good white flowered 'mosses' and 'Kingscote White' is a larger flowered pure white 'mossy' variety. 'Kathleen Pinsent' (encrusted) may be a *S. ligulata* × *S. callosa* hybrid, with 1 foot long stems and sprays of yellow eyed pink flowers. 'Myra' (Kabschia) is probably an *S. lilacina* hybrid, with compact, slow growing mounds of silvery rosettes and deep pink blossoms. 'Mrs. Piper' ('mossy') forms wide mats of soft green foliage studded freely with bright red flowers on 3 inch stems. 'Pearly King' is a similar 'mossy' with pearly white flowers. 'Pixie' is a compact growing 'mossy' with rose-red flowers. 'Riverslea' (*S. lilacina* × *S. porophylla*) is a Kabschia × Engleria hybrid, with silvery rosettes in compact mounds and purple-rose flowers

Saxifraga x jenkinsae, growing in tufa, is a free blooming Kabschia hybrid which forms a firm, pale-pink cushion of flowers.

on 3 inch stems. 'Salomonii' (*S. burseriana* × *S. marginata*) produces free growing silvery mats and 3 inch stems bearing large vase shaped white flowers that are pink in bud. 'Sir Douglas Haig' ('mossy') bears dark velvety-crimson flowers. 'Southside Seedling' is a comparatively new *S. cotyledon* hybrid with large silver rimmed rosettes and long sprays of white, intensely red spotted blossoms. ''Tumbling Waters' (*S. lingulata* × *S. longiflora*) is the finest large encrusted hybrid with huge silvered rosettes and magnificent 2 foot long plumes of white blossoms. 'Winston Churchill' ('mossy') bears soft pink flowers on 6 inch stems.

Cultivation With the exception of species in the section Hirculus, a few of the 'mossy' group, and *S. aizoides*, which need moist to wet conditions to thrive well, practically all saxifrages require a well drained site either in the rock garden, dry wall, raised bed, moraine, or in pots and pans in the alpine house. The Robertsonia species, typified by London pride, the Miscopetalum section, and such species as *S. hederacea*, require a shady site, the first mentioned does particularly well even in complete shade or in woodland. Kabschia species require particularly good drainage and are best grown in a scree or raised bed.

Flowering very early, they are ideally suited to alpine house culture where their delicate looking flowers may be appreciated unsullied by heavy rain and mud splash. Most of the encrusted group are ideal for the open rock garden, in rock crevices or dry walls; *S. cotyledon* and *longifolia* should always be grown in the latter habitat if at all possible. All the popular mossy hybrids and some of the species are good in the rock garden and are also suitable for paved areas and as ground cover for small bulbs. Generally speaking they will stand partial shade well and seem to thrive better if the site is not too sun drenched. Propagation is by seeds sown in pots or pans in early spring, placed in a cold frame, by division after flowering, or by offset rosettes inserted as cuttings in sand from spring to late summer.

Scabiosa (skay-bee-o-sa)

From the Latin *scabies*, itch, for which some of these plants were used as remedies, or from the Latin *scabiosus*, rough or scurfy, referring to the grey felting on the leaves of some species (*Dipsacaceae*). Scabious. This genus of 100 species of hardy biennial and perennial herbaceous plants, mainly from the Mediterranean region, includes several which are good decorative plants for the garden. *Scabiosa arvensis*, *S. columbaria* and *S. succisa*, are among the prettiest flowering wild plants

and are quite suited to garden cultivation. *S. succisa*, the devil's bit, is especially good as it has flowers of a bright blue color. In the plants in the *Dipsacaceae* family the so called flower is made up of a large number of small florets gathered into a head, or *capitulum*, somewhat as in *Compositae*.

Perennial species cultivated *S. arvensis* (syn. *Knautia arvensis*), field scabious, 1 foot, flowers bluish-lilac, July—August, Europe (including Britain). *S. caucasica*, 1—1½ feet, flowers mauve, blue or white, June to October, Caucasus; cvs. 'Clive Greaves', flowers mauve, large; 'Miss Willmott', large, white; 'Moonstone', large, lavender-blue. *S. columbaria*, 1—2 feet, lilac or blue-purple, July to September, Europe including Britain. *S. graminifolia*, 9 inches, leaves narrow, silvery-white, flowers pale mauve to rose, summer, southern Europe. *S. ochroleuca*, 2 feet, yellow, July to November, southeastern Europe; var. *webbiana*, 6 inches, flowers creamy-white. *S. succisa* (syn. *Succisa pratensis*), devil's bit, 1—2 feet, blue-purple or white, July to October, Europe including Britain.

Cultivation These plants all do well in most garden soils of high fertility. *S. caucasica* is suitable for the herbaceous border, but may also be grown to supply cut flowers, for which purpose its long clean stems make it very suitable. These plants should be lifted and divided every three or four years in the springtime. *S. craminifolia* and *S. ochroleuca webbiana* are suitable for the rock garden. *S. atropurpurea* can be raised from seed sown in February or March at a temperature of 60°F. Plant the seedlings in May to flower as annuals. Planting in July will cause them to behave as biennials. In the latter case, over winter them in a cold frame and plant out in April. They are good for cutting. Other species may be propagated by division of the clumps in March.

Sidalcea (sid-al-see-a)

A compound of two related genera, *Sida* and *Alcea*. The former comes from an ancient Greek name used by Theophrastus for the water lily, the latter from *Althaea*, the generic name for hollyhock (*Malvaceae*). These hardy perennial herbaceous plants belong to the same family as the hollyhock and the mallow. Their flowers have delicate papery petals in varying shades of pink and purple. There are 25 species, all from western North America.

1 The delicate blooms of Scabiosa caucasica are equally suitable for the herbaceous border or for use as cut flowers. Its blooms range from mauve and blue to pure white.
2 Sidalcea malvaeflora bears soft lilac blooms in mid summer. A number of reliable cultivars are available in a variety of colors.

Species cultivated S. candida, 2—3 feet, flowers white, summer, Colorado. S. malvaeflora, 1½—3 feet, rather twiggy in habit, flowers lilac, summer, California; var. listeri, pink. S. spicata, 1—3 feet, rosy-purple flowers, July—September, western North America. Some good cultivars include 'Brilliant', crimson; 'Elsie Heugh', pink, fringed flowers; 'Interlaken', pink; 'Puck', large clear pink flowers; 'Rev. Page Roberts', soft pink; 'Rose Queen', tall; 'William Smith', salmon-red.

Cultivation Ordinary, slightly sandy soil is suitable; the position should preferably have a sunny exposure. Plant in the autumn or spring, and lift and divide every three or four years. Propagation is by seeds sown in light soil in April, transplanting the seedlings in April or by division in October or March for the named varieties.

Silene (si-le-ne)

Probably from the Greek *sialon,* saliva, in reference to the gummy exudations on the stems which ward off insects (*Caryophyllaceae*). Catchfly. A genus of 100 species of annual, biennial and herbaceous perennials of the northern hemisphere and South Africa, having a wide range of color through white, pink and red to purple. Some make good rock plants, but some can only be considered as weeds and should not be planted.

Annual species cultivated S. armeria, 1—2 feet, flowers pink, summer, Europe. S. pendula, 12 inches, rose to white, summer, Europe.

Biennial species cultivated S. compacta, 1½ feet, flowers pink, summer, Russia, Asia Minor. S. rupestris, 4—6 inches, flowers white to pink, June to August, western Europe, Siberia.

Perennial species cultivated S. acaulis, cushion pink, moss campion, 2 inches, flowers pink, June, northern hemisphere. S. alpestris (syn. *Heliosperma alpestre*), 4 inches, white, summer, eastern Europe; var. plena, flowers double. S. laciniata (syn. *Melandrium laciniatum*), 8—10 inches, flowers scarlet, summer, United States. S. maritima, sea campion, 6 inches, flowers white, large, July to September, Europe including Britain; var. plena, flowers double. S. saxifraga, 6 inches, flowers white and brown, summer, Greece. S. schafta, 6—9 inches, flowers pink, summer and autumn, Caucasus. S. virginica (syn. *Melandrium virginicum*), fire pink, 1—1½ feet, flowers crimson, North America. S. zawadskyi (syn. *Melandrium zawadskyi*), 4—6 inches, flowers white, large, summer, Romania. Some good cultivars include S. pendula compacta, pink; rubervina, ruby red; 'Peach Blossom', single pink; 'Triumph', crimson-rose; 'Special Dwarf Mixture', double white through pink and lilac to crimson.

Cultivation The soil for annual and biennial species should be light and sandy, in a sunny bed or border. For perennials a sandy loam mixed with well rotted organic material is suitable. S. acaulis requires equal parts of loam, peat and stones and prefers a sunny crack or shelf on a rock garden, as does S. virginica. Planting is carried out in the spring, and lifting and replanting should be undertaken only when absolutely essential. Propagation for annuals is by seed sown in September, transplanting the seedlings when they are 1 inch high, and then planting them in their permanent positions in March for spring flowering, or by seed sown in April, transplanting to flowering positions when 1 inch high for summer blooming, or by sowing seed outside and thinning out in May. Perennials are propagated from seed sown in spring, in pans placed in cold frames, from cuttings and by division in spring.

Silphium (sil-fee-um)

The ancient Greek name referring to the resinous juice (*Compositae*). Rosinweed. A genus of 15 species of hardy perennial plants with the typical composite flower. The sap is resinous, and the plants are native to North America.

Species cultivated S. laciniatum, the compass plant, so-called because the leaves often face north and south, 6—8 feet, flowers yellow, July to August. S. perfoliatum, the cup plant, so-called because the leaves are joined together and form a cup round the stem, 4—6 feet, flowers yellow, July. Coarse textured plants, seldom used in gardens.

Cultivation These plants are easily grown in ordinary soil in a sunny border or bed. They should be planted between October and April, and every two or three years the plants should be lifted, divided and replanted. Propagation is by division of the roots, in October or March, or from seed sown in the spring.

Stachys (stak-is)

From the Greek *stachus,* a spike, alluding to the pointed inflorescences of this plant (*Labiatea*). A genus of 300 species of herbaceous perennials, annuals, subshrubs, with a few shrubby species, widely dispersed throughout the world. One tuberous rooted species, S. affinis, is the Chinese or Japanese artichoke. Some species are also known as wound wort or betony; they are closely related to the deadnettles (*Lamium*).

1 Silene maritima is the low growing, white flowered Sea Campion with a creeping habit.
2 Silene acaulis, the Moss Campion, forms a low pink cushion and prefers a sunny spot in the rock garden.
3 Silphium perfoliatum is called the Cup Plant because of its perfoliate leaves. It bears yellow daisy like flowers in midsummer.

1 Stachys macrantha, the Betony, is a summer flowering native of the Caucasus. 2 Thalictrum aquilegiifolium has delicately textured foliage and fluffy pinkish flowers like tiny daises.

Species cultivated S. affinis (syn. S. sieboldii, S. tuberifera), Chinese or Japanese artichoke, 1—1½ feet, roots edible, flowers pink, rarely seen, summer, China, Japan. S. coccinea, 2 feet, flowers scarlet, summer, Central America. S. corsica, 1 inch, a good rock garden plant, forms carpets of small leaves, flowers pale pink, almost stemless, all summer, Mediterranean region. S. lanata, lamb's ear, 1 foot, grey, densely woodly foliage, flowers small, purple, July, Caucasus to Persia. S. lavandulifolia, 6 inches, lavender leaved, flowers purplish-rose, July to August, Armenia. S. macrantha (syns. S. grandiflora, Betonica macrantha), betony, 1 foot, violet, May to July, Causasus. S. officinalis, bishop's wort, wood betony, to 3 feet, flowers purple, June to August, Europe.

Cultivation The hardy perennials thrive in ordinary soil in a warm sheltered border. The most attractive is S. corsica, which is a little tender and needs good drainage and sun. It is better under glass in winter. S. lanata is good for edgings to border or beds, and there is a form obtainable which does not flower. It should be planted in autumn or spring. Propagation is by division in autumn or spring.

Thalictrum (thal-ik-trum)

From the Greek *thaliktron*, a name used to describe a plant with divided leaves, possibly of the same family (*Ranunculaceae*). Meadow rue. A genus of 150 species of hardy perennials, herbaceous plants, mainly from north temperate regions but also represented in tropical South America, tropical Africa and South Africa. Those cultivated have elegant, fern like foliage and dainty flowers. They are most effective when planted in bold groups.

Species cultivated T. aquilegiifolium, 3—4 feet, flowers pale purple in fluffy panicles, May to July, Europe, northern Asia. T. chelidonii, 2—3 feet, flowers large, mauve, July to August, Himalaya. T. diffusiflorum, 2—3 feet, finely cut, gray-green foliage, sprays of clear lilac flowers, July and August, Tibet; a difficult plant to establish. T. dipterocarpum, 3—5 feet, leaves dainty, blue-green, smooth, flowers deep lavender with prominent yellow anthers borne on slender stems, July and August, western China; vars. *album,* a graceful white form; 'Hewitt's Double', bright violet-mauve, fully double flowers, freely produced. T. flavum, 2—3 feet, gray-green, glossy, finely cut foliage, soft yellow, feathery heads of flowers, July and August, Europe including Britain. T. glaucum (syn. T. speciosissimum), 5 feet, foliage glaucous, flowers yellow, summer, southern Europe, North Africa. T. kuisianum, 4 inches, foliage fern like, flowers rosy-purple, spring, Japan, rock garden or alpine house. T. minus (syn. T. adiantifolium), 1½—2 feet, grown purely for its decorative, maidenhair fern like foliage, borne on wiry stems which make it admirable for use with floral decorations, inconspicuous yellowish-green flowers in loose panicles, Europe. T. rocquebrunianum, 4 feet, stems and leaf stalks purplish, flowers lavender-blue in large heads, summer.

Cultivation Thalictrums will grow in almost any soil, preferably of reasonable depth, including those that are slightly alkaline, provided they do not bake dry. Plant them in full sun or dappled shade. Propagation is by seed or by division in the spring.

Tradescantia (trad-es-kan-tee-a)

Commemorating John Tradescant (died 1637), gardener to Charles I (*Commelinaceae*). A genus of 60 species of hardy perennial and greenhouse plants from North America and tropical South America. The hardy varieties are commonly called spiderwort. According to some botanists the garden plants grown under the name *T. virginiana* belong to a hybrid group known as *T. × andersoniana*.

Species cultivated *T. albiflora,* wandering Jew, trailing, fast growing greenhouse or house plant with shiny stems, swollen at the nodes, leaves narrow, pointed, South America; several variegated forms are known with cream and yellow striped leaves, green and white, or with faint red markings. *T. blossfeldiana,* creeping or trailing greenhouse or house plant, dark green leathery leaves, purple and whitely hairy beneath, Argentine. *T. fluminensis,* wandering Jew, trailing greenhouse or house plant, often confused with *T. albiflora,* leaves slender pointed, green, purplish-red beneath; several variegated forms, South America. *T. virginiana* spiderwort, etc., hardy perennial, 1½—2 feet, flowers violet-blue from June to September, eastern United States; vars. *alba,* a white form; *coerulea,* bright blue; 'Iris Prichard', white, shaded violet at the center; 'J. C. Weguelin', large azure-blue; 'Osprey', large, white, with feathery blue stamens; *rosea,* pink, *rubra,* dark ruby-red.

Cultivation The tender species and varieties require a minimum winter temperature of 55°F, and should be potted in March or April, in ordinary potting soil. Avoid a rich soil which may cause the leaves to turn green and lose their variegations. Hardy varieties can be grown in ordinary garden soil in sun or partial shade. Lift and divide in autumn or spring, every three or four years. Propagation of tender species is by cuttings taken at any season and inserted in pots of sandy soil in a warm propagating frame; they will root in two to three weeks. Hardy varieties may be increased by division in the spring.

Trollius (trol-lee-us)

From the German common name *trollblume,* or the Latin *trulleus,* a basin, referring to the flower shape (*Ranunculaceae*). Globe-flower. A genus of 25 species of hardy perennials with large buttercup like blooms, and usually with palmately lobed leaves. They are natives of northern temperate and arctic regions and are at their best besides a pool or stream.

Species cultivated *T. europaeus,* 1—2 feet, flowers lemon yellow, May and June, Europe; cvs. 'First Lancers', deep orange; 'Earliest of All', lemon yellow, April—June; 'Goldquelle', orange-yellow, May; 'Helios', citron yellow; 'Orange Princess', bright orange-yellow. *T. ledebourii* (syn. *T. chinensis*), 2—3 feet, flowers deep orange with bright orange stamens, June, northern China; a cultivar is 'Golden Queen', 2 feet, bright orange with conspicuous stamens. *T. pumilus,* 6—12 inches, buttercup yellow, rock garden, June and

1 *Verbascum dumulosum* thrives in a hot, dry place.
2 *Trollius europaeus* 'The Globe' is one of many cultivars.
3 *Tradescantia virginiana* is a good herbaceous perennial for damp soil.

July, Himalaya. *T. yunnanensis,* 1½—2 feet, flowers golden-yellow, western China.

Cultivation Plant in early autumn in semi shade or in full sun, provided the soil is deep, moist and loamy. Every three or four years, lift and divide them in autumn. Seed may also be sown, preferably on ripening, in pans or boxes of a loamy soil in September or April and placed in a shaded cold frame or stood in the open in the shade.

Verbascum (ver-bas-kum)

Possibly from the Latin *barba,* a beard, many species having a hairy or downy look (*Scrophulariaceae*). Mullein. A genus of 300 species of hardy herbaceous plants, mostly biennials or short lived perennials, from temperate parts of Europe and Asia.

Species cultivated *V. blattaria,* moth mullein, to 4 feet, flowers yellow or cream, Europe. *V. bombyciferum* (syns. *V.* 'Broussa', *V.* 'Brusa'), biennial, 4—6 feet, stem and leaves covered in silvery hairs, flowers golden-yellow, embedded in silvery hairs, June—July, western Asia Minor. *V. chaixii* (syn. *V. vernale*), 3 feet, stems purple, leaves covered with whitish hairs, flowers yellow, June—August, Europe. *V. dumulosum,* 1 foot, perennial, leaves gray felted, flowers lemon yellow, May—June, needs a hot, dry place or alpine house, Asia Minor. *V. nigrum* (syn. *V. vernale*), normally perennial, 2—3 feet, yellow, blotched reddish-brown, June to October, Europe. *V. olympicum,* perennial, 5—6 feet, leaves gray felted, flowers golden, June to September, Bithynia; several cultivars in shades of amber, terracotta, purple and yellow. *V. phoeniceum,* purple mullein, 3—5 feet; hybrids available in pink,

lilac, purple. *V. pulverulentum,* hoary mullein, leaves white hairy, flowers yellow, July, Europe. *V. thapsus,* common mullein, to 3 feet, very woolly, flowers yellow, summer, Europe, Asia.

Cultivation Verbascums grow easily in sunny positions and ordinary soil. Propagation of species is by seed sown in light soil outdoors in April. Hybrids, some of which are sterile, are increased by root cuttings in autumn or winter.

Veronica (ver-on-ik-a)

Origin doubtful, possibly named after St. Veronica (*Scrophulariaceae*). Speedwell. A genus of some 300 species of hardy perennials, annuals and subshrubs, mainly from northern temperate regions. Those described are hardy perennials, their flowers often borne in spikes. Dwarf kinds are suitable for the rock garden.

Species cultivated *V. agrestis,* procumbent speedwell, prostrate, flowers pink, annual weed, Europe. *V. chamaedrys,* germander speedwell, 1—1½ feet, bright blue, May onwards, Europe. *V. cinerea,* 6 inches, leaves gray, flowers pale blue, early

95

summer. *V. exaltata,* 5 feet, mauve in tall spikes, late summer. *V. fruticans* (syn. *V. saxatilis*), rock speedwell, 3 inches, sub-shrub, deep blue with red eye, late summer. *V. gentianoides,* 2 feet, pale blue in slender spikes, May—June; vars. *nana,* 1 foot; *variegata,* leaves variegated, flowers deeper blue. *V.* × *guthrieana,* 3 inches, flowers large, blue, hybrid. *V. hederifolia,* ivy leaved speedwell, similar to *V. agrestis,* Europe. *V. incana,* 1—2 feet, leaves gray, flowers dark blue, summer; var. *rosea,* pink. *V. longifolia,* 2—4 feet, lilac-blue, late summer; var. *subsessilis,* royal blue. *V. pectinata,* 3 inches, mat forming, leaves gray, flowers deep blue with white eye, May; var. *rosea,* pink. *V. prostrata,* 6 inches, creeping, blue, summer; vars, 'Mrs. Holt', pink; *rosea,* rosy-pink; 'Shirley Blue', deep blue; 'Trehane', leaves golden, flowers light blue. *V. spicata,* 2 feet, bright blue, late summer; vars. *alba,* white; many varieties in blue, purple, and pink. *V. scutellata,* marsh speedwell, creeping, flowers pale blue, pink or white, Europe, North America. *V. teucrium,* 1—2 feet, lavender-blue, late summer; vars. 'Blue Fountain', 2 feet, intense blue; 'Royal Blue', 1½ feet. *V. virginica,* 4—5 feet, light blue, late summer; var. *alba,* white. *V. whitleyi,* 3—4 inches, tufted, blue with white eye, June to August.

Cultivation Veronicas will grow in ordinary soil and a sunny position. Propagation is by division in August or in spring, or by seed sown in the open in spring in light soil and in part shade.

1 *Viola cornuta* 'Jersey Gem' has sturdy royal purple flowers.
2 *Viola tricolor hortensis* 'Ardrossan Gem' is marked with yellow.
3 *Viola odorata* is the Sweet Violet.
4 *Veronica teucrium* 'Trehane' blooms in late summer.

Viola (vi-o-la)

An old Latin name for violet (*Violaceae*). A genus of some 500 species of hardy perennials, mainly from northern temperate regions, including violas, pansies and violets of which there are many hybrids and strains.

Species cultivated *V. adunca,* hooked spur violet, to 4 inches, violet or lavender with white eye, spring, North America. *V. arvensis* field pansy, 6 inches, cream, Europe, Asia, annual weed. *V. cornuta,* horned violet, 9—12 inches, flowers violet, June to August, Pyrenees; cultivars, including the 'Violettas', derived mainly from this species, are available in shades of yellow, plum-purple, rosy-lilac, blue and white with a yellow eye. *V. cucullata,* 6 inches, white, veined lilac, April to June, North America. *V.* × *florairensis,* 4 inches, mauve and yellow, spring and summer, hybrid. *V. gracilis,* 4—6 inches, deep violet, April to August, Balkans, Asia Minor vars. *alba,* white; 'Black Knight', purplish-black; *lutea,* golden-yellow; *major,* violet. *V. hispida,* Rouen pansy, to 8 inches, violet, summer, Europe. *V. labradorica,* 4—6 inches, porcelain blue, summer, North America. *V. odorata,* see Violet. *V. palmata,* 6 inches, violet-purple, summer, North America. *V. rupestris,*

Teesdale violet, to 2 inches, bluish-violet, Asia, Europe, North America. *V. saxatilis,* 4—8 inches, violet, summer, Europe, Asia Minor. *V.* × *wittrockiana,* see Pansy.

Cultivation Violas do best in a moist, well drained soil and in light shade. Propagation of cultivars is by cuttings rooted in late summer in sandy soil in a cold, shaded frame. Species and strains are raised from seed sown in late summer in light soil in a cold, shaded frame.

Violet

Viola odorata, the sweet violet, is a hardy perennial, parent of the florist's violets, many of them sweetly scented. The soil should be rich and moist but well drained. Plant the crowns in the open in a sheltered, shady position in April, or in September for winter flowering in a cold sunny frame. Propagation is by runners removed in April. Other runners that are produced during the summer months should be removed and discarded.

Named cultivars include: 'Couer d'Alsace', pink; 'Czar', blue; 'De Parme', pale lavender, double; 'Governor Herrick', deep blue; 'Marie Louise', mauve, double, good for frame cultivation; 'La France', violet-blue; 'Princess of Wales', large violet-blue; 'Sulphurea', creamy-yellow; 'White Czar', single white.